the EDINB visitor guide

Colin Baxter Photography, Grantown-on-Spey, Scotland

CONTENTS

Edinburgh Castle and City from Salisbury Crags

HOW TO USE THIS GUIDE

The Edinburgh Visitor Guide is split into two chapters. Entries are arranged alphabetically, and contain practical information on facilities, opening times, admission, directions, contact telephone number and website plus a short description. A typical entry looks like this one for Edinburgh Castle (below).

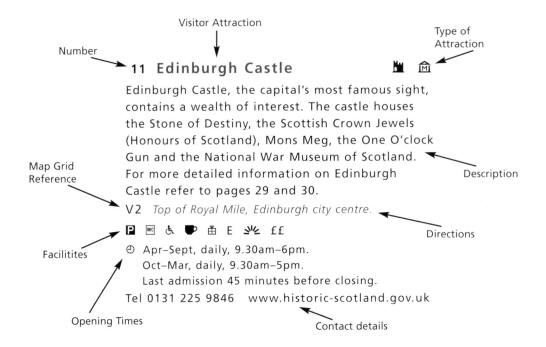

About the Symbols
A number of symbols have been used throughout the book to represent types of attractions, facilities and whether the entry is associated with the National Trust for Scotland or Historic Scotland. You can find a list of these symbols on the inside cover of this book.

Using the Maps
All entries are clearly marked on colour-coded maps (on pages 18 & 19, 20 & 21 & 68) using the reference number next to the title (in the case of Edinburgh Castle, 11). You can also use the map grid reference (V2) to find the location quickly.

Using the Indexes
Two indexes at the back of the book provide easy reference; the first is ordered by type of attraction, and the second is alphabetical by title.

Special Text
A number of special features appear throughout the guide, which highlight areas and places of historical interest, events and attractions.

VISITOR INFORMATION

Tourist Information Centres offer a wealth of information to anyone visiting Edinburgh and the surrounding area. They can advise visitors on events, attractions, festivals and activities. Passes can be arranged for coach and walking tours in the city. The centres carry a selection of books, guidebooks, maps and souvenirs. You can also book accommodation in Edinburgh and throughout Scotland through the centres and some offer a service for foreign currency exchange.

YEAR ROUND TOURIST INFORMATION CENTRES

Edinburgh
3 Princes Street
Edinburgh, EH2 2QP
Tel: 0845 22 55 121 (UK)
Tel: 44 (0)1506 832 121 (outside UK)
Web: www.edinburgh.org
Email: info@visitscotland.com
Open: all year round

Edinburgh International Airport
Tourist Information Desk
Main Concourse
Edinburgh Airport
EH12 9DN
Tel: 0870 040 0007
Email: info@visitscotland.com
Open: all year round

North Berwick
Quality Street
North Berwick
EH39 4HJ
Tel: 01620 892197
Email: info@visitscotland.com
Open: all year round

Dunfermline
1 High Street
Dunfermline
KY12 7DL
Tel: 01383 720999
Email: dunfermline@visitfife.com
Open: all year round

Forth Bridges
Queensferry Lodge Hotel
North Queensferry
KY11 1HP
Tel: 01383 417759
Email: forthbridges@visitfife.com
Open: all year round

SEASONAL TOURIST INFORMATION CENTRES

Linlithgow
Burgh Halls
The Cross, Linlithgow
EH49 8RE
Tel: 01506 844600
Email: info@visitscotland.com
Closed Nov–Mar

Old Craighall
Old Craighall Junction, A1
EH21 8RE
Tel: 0131 653 6172
Email: info@visitscotland.com
Closed Nov–Mar

Newtongrange
Scottish Mining Museum
Newtongrange
EH22 4QN
Tel: 0131 663 4262
Email: info@visitscotland.com
Closed Nov–Mar

EDINBURGH

I first saw Scotland's capital city as I drove over bleak Soutra Moor 12 miles to its south. Lothian's 'heavy-laden grainfields' lay stretched out before me, and in the distance the thin streak of blue of the Firth of Forth. Over to my left the rolling Pentland Hills, and far to my right Traprain's ridged hump and the rocky cone of North Berwick Law, mere dimples on the flat land.

But it was the hills in front of me that caught my eye most. Seven of them, all clustered together. I would later learn their names - Blackford, Braid, Calton, Castle, Corstorphine, Craiglockhart, and foremost of all Edinburgh's 'mountain in the city', Arthur's Seat – but in that instant I understood why this city on the north-west fringe of Europe has been likened to the 'Eternal City' far away in the Mediterranean sun – for there were Rome's seven hills, here in Scotia's capital.

I strained my eyes closer. There was the ancient castle atop its rocky perch, looking for all the world like a mother hen clutching her chicks about her. But what was the hill to its right? The Acropolis? Here in wind-swept Edinburgh? Only later, as I explored Calton Hill with its curious neo-classical follies, would I appreciate why Edinburgh came to be known as 'the Athens of the North'.

Many visiting Edinburgh today come by road. Few now approach it from the sea, through the ancient port of Leith, the historic 'gateway' to Scotland. More's the pity, for to have sailed up the Firth of Forth and gazed towards mighty Arthur's Seat and the ridgy back of the ancient city must surely have made the eye of many an old salt moisten.

For those arriving by rail, these distant vistas are denied them, for they emerge blinking from the depths of Waverley Station right into Edinburgh's throbbing heart. Immediately they become conscious of the city's split personality. There, high on its sloping ridge, the riotous confusion of stone and spires that is the medieval Old Town; and facing it across the valley the ordered symmetry of the New Town – well, it was new when begun in George III's reign over 200 years ago. 'Old' and 'New' are as different as night and day, the one dark and haunting, the other light and welcoming. They are Robert Louis Stevenson's 'Dr Jekyll and Mr Hyde' wrought in stone.

EARLY HISTORY

We do not know when humans first gazed upon the hills and green valleys that would one day become Edinburgh. Pot-sherds from the Bronze Age 3000 years ago have recently been discovered on the Castle Rock, and tell-tale signs of Iron-Age forts built by the native

Britons can still be made out on the slopes of Arthur's Seat. The area was certainly well inhabited in AD 79 when the Romans marched by on their way to fight the Caledonian tribes far to the north. The legionaries built their barrack-blocks and bath-houses at Inveresk and Cramond, down by the Forth where they could be supplied from the sea. A morning's sail up-river took them to Bo'ness and the east end of the Antonine Wall, built on the orders of Emperor Antoninus Pius in the 140s; it became Imperial Rome's most northerly frontier and today visitors can still follow it across Scotland's central belt from Forth to Clyde.

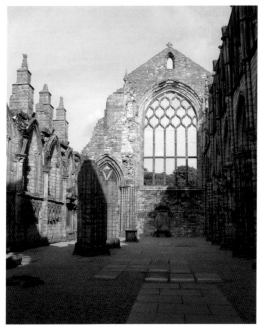

Holyrood Abbey was founded by King David I in 1128

THE DARK AGES

In the Dark Ages, following the fall of Rome, the Britons staged a comeback. By 600, a great king rejoicing in the name of Mynyddog Mwynfawr 'the magnificent' held sway from the summit of the castle rock, then known as Din Eidyn, 'the stronghold of Eidyn'; though who Eidyn was is a mystery. But when Mynyddog and his warband rode down from the rock to do battle in far-off Yorkshire with the Angles, recent invaders from Europe, they lost disastrously. The Angles chased them back to Din Eidyn, captured it and renamed it Edinburgh, the English name it has retained ever since.

The Old Town of Edinburgh emerges onto the pages of history only from the early twelfth century. It actually began as two towns – the royal burgh of Edinburgh, founded in the shadow of the royal castle by King David I, and the ecclesiastical burgh of Canongate, established by the Augustinian canons of Holyrood Abbey. The castle at the top of the ridge and the abbey at its foot were linked by the *via regis* or 'royal way', known today as the Royal Mile. The castle was intended as a residence as well as a fortress, but it wasn't long before the royal family were choosing to stay in the abbey's more sheltered guesthouse rather than on the exposed castle rock. In time they ousted the canons altogether and made the old abbey into a 'house of Kings', the Palace of Holyroodhouse.

The first inhabitants of Edinburgh were incomers mostly, sporting names belying their foreign roots, like Bartholemew, Mortimer, Michael of Flanders and William de Dederyck. They were invited by the king to cross the North Sea and settle chiefly because of their skills as merchants and craftsmen. These early burgesses formed a corporation to administer the town's affairs and protect their jealously-guarded royal privileges, and they appointed one of their number to be their head burgess, or provost. Nine centuries later and Edinburgh still has its City Council and Lord (sometimes even Lady) Provost.

For the first 200 years of its existence, Edinburgh played 'second fiddle' to Berwick-upon-Tweed, then Scotland's chief town and port. But once Edward I of England, 'Hammer of the Scots', crossed the Tweed and slaughtered its townsfolk in 1296, Berwick declined and Edinburgh came increasingly to the fore. The busy High Street became the focus of the political and religious life of the nation, where kings and knaves, bishops and beggars rubbed shoulders. As you stand by the Mercat Cross, just imagine the racket on market day, the merchants 'wheeling and dealing' in the open, the taverns around filled with raucous noise, and from high up in the tenements the cries of 'gardy-loo', closely followed by the sight, and smell, of chamber-pots being emptied onto the people thronging the cramped closes and narrow wynds below. And everywhere rotting dung in the gutters, and rats infesting the sewers beneath.

Through the fourteenth and fifteenth centuries, the town grew in prosperity, helped in large part by King Robert the Bruce's decision, shortly before his death in 1329, to grant to the burgesses control over the bustling port of Leith, with its valuable 'customs', or taxes levied on all imports and exports. Edinburgh also grew in size. In 1335, we read of a 'new street', later called 'the Cowgate', in the valley of the Cowgate Burn to the south of the town, close to where the Black Friars had built their convent in 1230. The process of encroaching on Edinburgh's 'green belt' had begun, and the poor cows were left to find another watering-hole.

PRINCIPAL BURGH OF THE KINGDOM

In 1482 James III declared Edinburgh to be 'the more principal burgh of our kingdom', and his continued presence there (he seldom set foot out of the place) helped to make the burgh 'de facto' Scotland's capital. Yet more people gravitated to the city, and soon the plague-bound, fire-prone city, constrained within its tight defensive corset, the King's Wall, was bursting at the seams. The great aristocratic families, wishing to be close to their sovereign, built their stately new townhouses on the available land in Canongate, whilst the wealthiest Edinburgh burgesses relocated to new and grander houses in the Cowgate, where by 1500, according to one who visited, 'nothing is mean or tasteless, but all is magnificent'; plus ça change!

Then disaster befell the nation, and the citizens of Edinburgh trembled and feared the worst. In 1513 their king, James IV, was killed fighting the English at Flodden, in Northumberland, and with him fell many of his subjects, the 'flower of Scotland'. In haste, the City Fathers built a new wall to shield them from the 'auld enemy'; they called it the Flodden Wall, and much of it is there still. The wealthy burgesses who had so recently escaped the narrow confines of the old wall now found themselves enveloped yet again inside another stone girdle.

For the next 30 years, Edinburghers lurked behind their new wall, but although English armies came – most threateningly in 1544 when the Earl of Hertford almost succeeded in taking the castle – they soon went away again. Edinburgh survived as capital city – it was formally declared as much by James V in 1532 – where Berwick two centuries earlier had not.

THE REFORMATION

Now a new struggle manifested itself, the fight for the nation's soul. The Reformation that had swept across the Continent of Europe now appeared in Scotland, and when the man chiefly responsible, John Knox, became the first Protestant minister of the High Kirk of St Giles in 1559, the die was cast. In the following year, Parliament, sitting in the city's Tolbooth next door to St Giles', passed the Act of Reformation; Catholicism was now forbidden. Knox spent the remaining years of his life haranguing his congregation from the pulpit on the evils of 'popery'. He is even said to have lectured them from the box window of John Knox's House, in the High Street, though there is no evidence that he ever lived there. The fiery preacher died of a stroke shortly after giving one such sermon in St Giles' in 1572 and was buried in the graveyard outside.

Religious persuasions, though, weren't so easily changed, and the struggle between Catholics and Protestants continued to divide the nation. In the short term it brought civil war, as the Catholic supporters of the exiled Mary Queen of Scots fought those loyal to her son, James VI. For three long years, between 1571 and 1573, Mary's men held out in the mighty castle of Edinburgh, now and then firing down on the citizens below; on one such occasion, a cannonball blew the baskets in the Fish Market, near St Giles', so high into the air that their contents landed on the rooftops of the ten-storey-high houses nearby. Eventually a huge artillery bombardment brought much of the eastern side of the castle crashing down and left a gaping hole in the ancient palace where Mary had given birth to her son just seven years earlier. The castle governor, Sir William

Kirkcaldy of Grange, had no option but to surrender and was ignominiously hauled behind a cart through the crowded streets to the Mercat Cross and beheaded on 'the Maiden', Edinburgh's guillotine (now on display in the Museum of Scotland). His severed head was then impaled on a spike on the ruined castle walls as a warning to all who dared to follow in his footsteps. Only when Queen Elizabeth of England had Mary beheaded at Fotheringhay, in Northamptonshire, in 1587 did the bitterness abate.

Then came that day in 1603 when James VI received the news in his bedchamber at Holyroodhouse that his Aunt Elizabeth, the 'Virgin Queen', was dead and he was now James I of England also. Down the road to London he went with almost indecent haste, the 'great and grand' of Scottish society following in his wake. Holyroodhouse fell silent, the lights in the grand townhouses of Canongate went out, and Edinburgh lost that 'capital' feeling. Other than one fleeting return by the ageing King James in 1617, and two equally short visits by Charles I, in 1633 and 1641, that was the last Edinburgh saw of its sovereigns for the next 200 years.

Charles I's coronation visit in 1633 brought with it joy and anger in equal measure. The City Fathers spared no expense to welcome their king, and the celebrations were a wonder to behold; they included an elaborate tableau depicting Charles' royal lineage

Mercat Cross, High Street

back to Fergus mac Erc, the legendary founder of the Scottish nation. His Majesty entered into the spirit by ordering the building of a new Parliament Hall, beside St Giles', to replace the old Tolbooth. But it was his plan for St Giles' Kirk itself that so enraged his northern subjects. The Scots had got rid of bishops in 1592, and didn't want their high kirk turned into a cathedral. Charles would have none of it, the bishop moved in and the congregation walked out. That single act led directly to the signing of the National Covenant in the kirk of the Greyfriars in 1638 which put king and country on a collision course. Before he knew it, the unbending Charles was facing civil war in all three of his kingdoms, Scotland, England and Ireland. His execution in London by Oliver Cromwell in 1649, far from solving the constitutional crisis, simply changed the leading characters, and in September 1650 Cromwell invaded Scotland; by Christmas he was sitting warming himself in Edinburgh Castle.

Cromwell soon returned south but his 'Roundheads' remained for another ten years, ruling the land first from their temporary headquarters high up in the medieval castle, and then from a purpose-built new fort down in the port of Leith, where they could be more safely supplied from the sea. Today, only the main entrance gate into 'Oliver's Fort' remains, hidden away behind a warren of warehouses. When Charles II returned to his throne in 1660, he too was determined to make his mark with a new architectural statement, and although he never once visited Edinburgh, he contributed to its architectural greatness with a splendid new Palace of Holyroodhouse, the building visitors admire today.

Despite all these upheavals and uncertainties, Edinburgh retained its supremacy as capital city and home of the nation's Parliament. The Honours of Scotland, the royal regalia, safely stored in the castle, now assumed an even greater importance, representing the absent sovereign at sittings of Parliament. Before each session, the Crown, Sceptre and Sword of State were brought down from the fortress in an elaborate procession known as the 'Ryding of Parliament', and

an act could only receive the royal assent when the king's commissioner touched the parchment with the Sceptre. The last time that occurred was on 16 January 1707, when the members voted to pass the Act of Union, uniting the two sovereign states of Scotland and England. Down the road to London disappeared the lucky 61 members of the new United Kingdom Parliament, and into Parliament Hall moved the lawyers and advocates; they are there to this day.

Even with the loss of Parliament, and the departure for London of many of its more affluent citizens, Edinburgh continued to flourish. It became the banking as well as the national capital. The Bank of Scotland, the country's first and founded in 1695, was now joined by the rival Royal Bank of Scotland, which opened its first premises in 1727. These were the first banks in the world to successfully issue paper currency. Soon banknotes were passing over the counters of the wigmakers and jewellers, being used to hire sedan chairs and the services of fencing masters.

Not even the troubles visited on Edinburgh by the Jacobite upheavals of the first half of the eighteenth century could dent the city's pride or halt its progress. Indeed, Bonnie Prince Charlie's brief stay at Holyroodhouse in the early days of the '45 Rising, when the strains of courtly life could be heard once more echoing around the walls, held out the promise of

Palace of Holyroodhouse

what might be if the house of Stewart, or the house of Hanover for that matter, were to return once again to Edinburgh.

THE ENLIGHTENMENT

By the time the Stewart hopes were trodden into the mud of Culloden in 1746, Edinburgh was beginning to enjoy the benefits of Union, particularly the increased trade with the American colonies and the burgeoning British Empire. The city grew once more, first in a modest way with the building of George Square to the south of the Cowgate, and then to the north in the 1760s in the most spectacular fashion possible. Out beyond the Nor' Loch (where Princes Street gardens are today, and better known as a repository for worried cats and drowned dogs than for tasty fish

and eels) and over the green fields spread Edinburgh's 'New Town', its classical lines and graceful curves contrasting hugely with the higgledy-piggledy wynds and closes of the 'Old'. Once out of the Old Town's stranglehold, there was no holding back the inhabitants. Across the plains they built their squares and crescents, north and west to the Water of Leith, 'Edinburgh's powerhouse', east to the 'Acropolis' of Calton Hill and beyond.

Edinburgh Old and New now became the centre of the great 'Age of the Scottish Enlightenment', a dazzling period of sustained intellectual thought and artistic creativity that had the eyes of the world gazing in admiration; even the great Voltaire proclaimed: 'It is to Edinburgh that we must look for our intellectual tastes.' The city gave birth to such 'stars' of the Enlightenment as

Charlotte Square, New Town

David Hume (b 1711), the philosopher who put the 'light' into Enlightenment, scientists of the calibre of James Hutton (b 1726), the father of modern geology, the renowned artists Allan Ramsay (b 1713) and Henry Raeburn (b 1756), and that towering figure from the world of literature, Sir Walter Scott (b 1771). They have been followed since by equally great minds, not least James Clerk Maxwell, universally regarded as the father of modern physics, born in India Street in 1831, and that other literary giant, Robert Louis Stevenson, born just around the corner in Heriot Row in 1850.

Stevenson travelled the world in search of a better life, and yet the lad from 17 Heriot Row could never leave behind his native land, and the city where he was born on 13 November 1850.

If his father had had his way, young Robert would have entered the family engineering business. But designing lighthouses wasn't for him; all he wanted to do was write. The many days the sickly child spent in his bed in Edinburgh's New Town helped him

on his way. As he stared out of his bedroom window across the Firth of Forth, he dreamed what all boys dream of – adventure, 'goodies and baddies' and deeds of derring-do. And they all came wonderfully together in his first novel, *Treasure Island*. That rattling yarn, published before Stevenson reached 30, launched him on his chosen career. By his death, at the tragically early age of 44, he had become the best-loved storyteller of his day.

Stevenson wrote *Treasure Island* in Scotland; and yet Scotland had no place in it. Only when he left its shores did he draw upon his knowledge and love of his native land and the city of his birth. *The Strange Case of Dr Jekyll and Mr Hyde*, the Edinburgh schizophrenic based on the sinister figure of Deacon brodie, Stevenson wrote on the south coast of England, and St Ives, set in Edinburgh during the Napoleonic Wars, at his island home on Samoa, where he died on 3 December 1894. It was as if the further Robert got from Edinburgh, the more nostalgic he became, and the more powerfully he wrote about it. Those early years spent abed, fighting wars on his counterpane and awaiting Leerie the Lamplighter, have given to children of all ages, then and today, countless hours of pleasure.

Robert Louis Stevenson died on the distant island of Samoa in the Pacific. Perhaps his poor health was the result of breathing in the polluted smoke belching from all the chimneys that had by then sprouted up all over the city. So smoky did Edinburgh become that its citizens nicknamed it 'auld

Reekie' ('old Smokey'). By 1850, Edinburgh was certainly a very different vision from the one imagined by the creators of the New Town a century earlier.

THE INDUSTRIAL REVOLUTION

During the nineteenth century, Edinburgh became noted not just for its 'banks' but for three other 'Bs' too – books, biscuits and beer. From the time Scotland's first books rolled off Chapman and Millar's presses, in Edinburgh's Cowgate, in 1508, the pivotal role of the city in the world of printing and publishing was secured. Edinburgh has subsequently given the world the *Encyclopaedia Britannica* (1768) and such famous publishing houses as Blackwood's and Constable's. The 'heavy-laden grainfields' of Lothian provided the flour from which biscuit-manufacturers such as Crawford's and McVitie's made their world-famous oatcakes and shortbread. And the artesian wells of Holyrood supplied the water with which William Younger began brewing his beer in 1749; the company he established has since transmogrified into the giant Scottish & Newcastle Breweries.

MODERN TIMES

By the dawn of the twentieth century, Edinburgh's population had exploded to 400,000, a three-fold increase in just 100 years. Then came the Great War, and many of the city's menfolk marched off to the Flanders' killing fields, among them the entire Heart of Midlothian football team. The nearby presence of the Forth Rail Bridge (opened 1890) and the Rosyth Naval Depot (built 1904) also brought the horror of war home to the citizens left behind. In April 1916, a German Zeppelin appeared over Leith and headed inland. In desperation, the garrison in the castle fired the One O'Clock Gun, the only time that historic time-piece has been fired in anger, forcing the airship to drop its payload near Lothian Road and head for home. Visitors to the Scottish National War Memorial in Edinburgh Castle can see a stained-glass window depicting that event.

Between the two World Wars, Edinburgh took the opportunity to demolish much of its crumbling housing stock in the Old Town and rehouse its inhabitants anew in the 'greenbelt'. From Cramond to Currie, in Sighthill and Saughton, rose the neat bungalows and council-house estates, art-deco roadhouses and shopping arcades, radiating out from the city centre like the spokes of a bicycle wheel. The advent of the tram, omnibus and motor car were fast making city-centre living unnecessary. Every citizen, though, would have had a grandstand view in September 1939 of the first 'dog-fight' fought between British and German aircraft, which ended with the downing of the first German bomber on British soil, in an East Lothian field.

Since World War II, 'auld Reekie' has largely cleaned up its act and

The Scottish Parliament Building, Holyrood

become a vibrant modern city. In 1997 the people of Scotland voted to have their own Parliament once again. On 1 July, 1999 the dream was realised when the Queen opened the Scottish Parliament, in its temporary site in the Assembly Hall on the Mound. On 9 October 2004 the Queen opened the new Scottish Parliament building at the foot of the Royal Mile opposite the Palace of Holyroodhouse.

Five hundred years ago, Edinburgh had barely 5000 inhabitants; today there are over 500,000 of us. And when the Festival-goers are in town, there are as many again – at least it feels like it! The thousands who flock to the nation's capital for the month of August will find a city of contrast, of contradiction – of ramshackle 'Old' and classical 'New', of touristy centre and tawdry suburbs, the 'Edinburgh' of the refined and the 'Embra' of ordinary folk.

The Edinburgh International Festival has only been going for just over 50 years, yet it feels it could be 500 – a 'tradition' already. That's the essence of the city – a thousand years of history and still going strong, a fondness, obsession even, for its past but with its eyes firmly fixed on the future.

Chris Tabraham

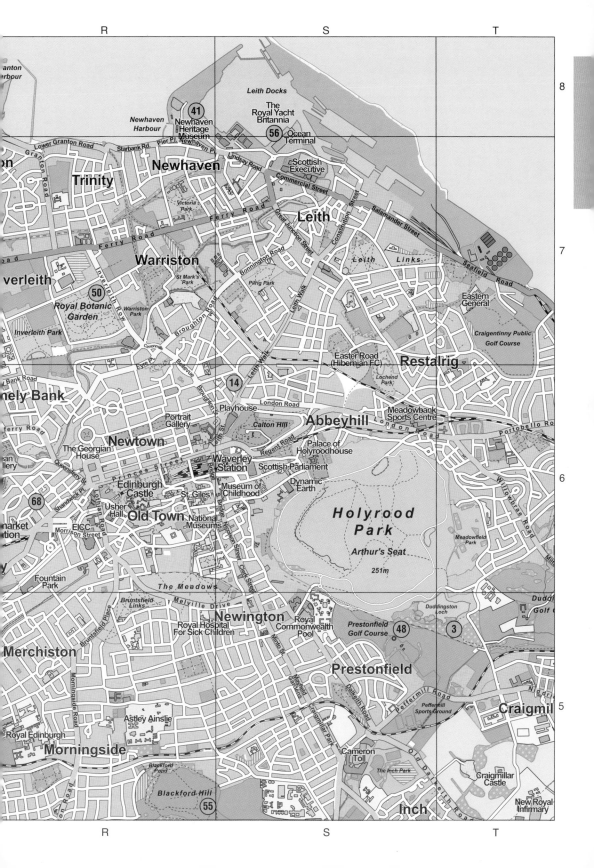

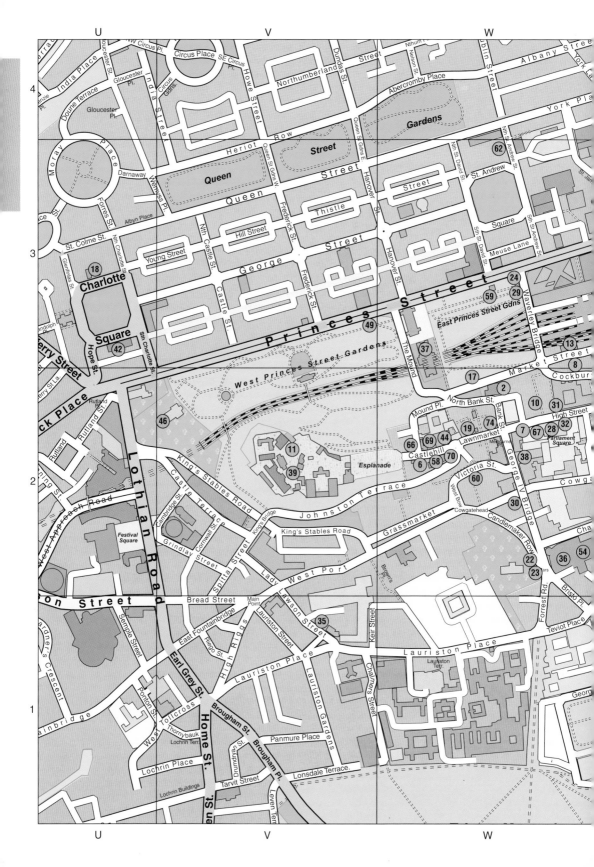

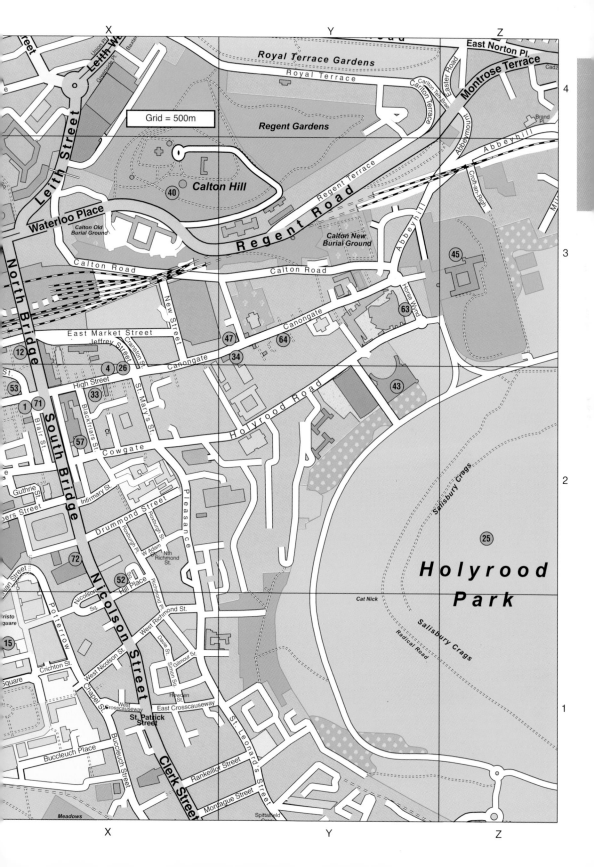

ATTRACTIONS IN EDINBURGH

1 Auld Reekie Prestige Tour ★

Costumed guides take you on walking tours back into Edinburgh's grisly past with terrifying stories of the characters that once walked the streets of the city. Visit the underground vaults, pagan temple and an exhibition on Medieval torture instruments.

X2 *Tours leave from the Tron Kirk on the Royal Mile.*

£££

⊕ Day tours from 12.30pm–5.30 pm, duration 50 minutes. Evening tours from 7pm; last tour 10.30pm, duration 1.5 hours. Extra charge for exhibition.

Tel 0131 557 4700   www.auldreekietours.co.uk

2 Bank of Scotland Museum on the Mound 🏛

Located in the Bank of Scotland's Head Office building on the Mound, this small but unique museum tells the story of three centuries of Scottish banking. Established in 1695, the Bank of Scotland is the first and oldest of all the Scottish banks. The museum showcases the Bank's history, from its modest beginnings, to the modern hi-tech era. On display are a range of treasures including a selection of Scotland's earliest coins, a 17th-century bullion 'kist' used to store cash, forged bank notes and a re-creation of a Victorian branch.

W2 *Bank of Scotland Head Office on the Mound.*

E FREE

⊕ Closed for refurbishment, reopening late summer 2006. Call or check website for details.

Tel 0131 529 1288

www.hbosplc.com/abouthbos/history/museum

3 Bawsinch and Duddingston Loch 🦆

A haven for birds and wildlife two miles from the centre of Edinburgh. It features fresh-water ponds, marshland with reedbeds, willow and poplar woodland. The reserve has a number of notable species of birds and rare plants. Otter and water vole have also been seen.

T5 *Southern end of Holyrood Park.*

🧎 FREE

⊕ Open access to the north shore and to the cavalry ground to the east. SWT members can obtain key for further access.

Tel 0131 312 7765   www.swt.org.uk

4 Brass Rubbing Centre ★

The centre offers a 'hands-on' approach in learning about design over the decades with a collection of replicas moulded from ancient Pictish stone, rare Scottish and medieval church brasses. Experienced staff show visitors how to do their own brass rubbings.

X2 *Historical Trinity Apse opposite the Museum of Childhood, Royal Mile, Edinburgh city centre.*

🏛 ££

⊕ Apr–Sept, Mon–Sat, 10am–5pm; Festival opening: Sun, 12 noon–5pm. Last rubbings 1 hour before closing.

Tel 0131 556 4364

www.cac.org.uk

5 Bruntsfield Links Golfing Society 🚩18

Fifth oldest golf club in the world, dating back to 1761. This 18 hole course of 6407 yards and par 71 is not a links but a parkland course in the suburbs of Edinburgh. The greens are large and undulating in character and the surroundings make it a pleasant course to play.

P7 *Off A90 (Forth Road Bridge), three miles NW of city centre at Davidson Mains*

🅿 🚻 🏛 ✕ 💳 £££

⊕ Telephone to book.

Tel 0131 336 1479

www.sol.co.uk/b/bruntsfieldlinks

6 Cadies and Witchery Tours ★

Witchery Tours take a light-hearted look at Edinburgh's dark side including tales of witchcraft, plague and torture. Ghostly guides or cadies, 18th-century messenger boys who would show visitors round the narrow closes, will take you through the eerie alleyways and courtyards of the Old Town, while 'jump-ooters' will provide ghastly appearances. Booking is essential.

W2 *Tours leave from outside the Witchery Restaurant at Castlehill, top of the Royal Mile.*

💳 £££

⊕ Evening tours, times vary. Booking essential, telephone 10am–6pm.

Tel 0131 225 6745   www.witcherytours.com

CALTON HILL

If there is one area of the city that can claim for Edinburgh the accolade 'Athens of the North' it is Calton Hill. The grassy height dominating the east end of the city centre abounds with edifices that look for all the world as though they should be shimmering in the Mediterranean heat, not shivering in the Caledonian cool. Prince Albert, according to Queen Victoria, 'felt sure the Acropolis could not be finer'.

Ancient Greece came to Calton Hill in the early 19th century. As the green fields to the north of the Old Town disappeared beneath the elegant Georgian streets of the New Town, it wasn't long before Calton Hill was being eyed as the perfect theatrical backdrop to the neo-classical architecture advancing towards it.

The explosion of building began in earnest with Wellington's great victory at Waterloo in 1815. Up till then, all the hill could boast was a modest Observatory House (1776), and the inimitable Nelson Monument (1807), the admiral's upturned telescope recreated in stone. Then came Waterloo and that collective rush of blood to the City Fathers' heads. The domed 'temple' of the City Observatory appeared first, in 1818. Twelve years later two circular monuments, loosely based on Lysicrates' tomb in Athens, concluded the vision; the eminent philosopher, Professor Dugald Stewart, may well have approved of his, but goodness knows what the national bard, Robert Burns, thought of his!

In between came Edinburgh's answer to the Parthenon, the National Monument. Begun in a blaze of glory during George IV's visit in 1822, the project fizzled out seven years later; just 12 giant columns had been built for £42,000!

But the National Monument wasn't a waste. It impressed then, and it continues to impress today. It also helped the young William Henry Playfair, who designed it, get his architectural eye in, and he went on to create some of Edinburgh's finest landmarks.

7 City of the Dead Graveyard Tour ★

This walking tour combines history with comedy, threading its way through the dark and sinister wynds of Edinburgh's historical Royal Mile before entering the walls of Greyfriars Graveyard. One section of the cemetery, The Covenanter's Prison, is kept locked after repeated attacks by an entity named the 'Mackenzie Poltergeist' after Sir George Mackenzie, the King's Advocate, who is buried at Greyfriars and is one of the most documented supernatural cases in history. The 'City of the Dead' tour have access to the key of the Covenanter's Prison and since these tours started in 2001, there have been many unexplained incidents centred on the prison. Not for the nervous or faint-hearted.

W2 *Tours leave the Royal Mile, in the vicinity of St. Giles' Cathedral.*

WC ££££

Office hours: all year round,10am–10pm. Tours: nightly, Apr–Oct at 8.30pm, 9.15pm & 10pm; Nov–May, 7.30pm & 8.30pm.

Tel 0131 225 9044

www.blackhart.uk.com

CITY WATERFRONT, LEITH & NEWHAVEN

Half-way down Leith Walk is a public house called the Boundary Bar; the brass
plaque on the wall declares that you are on the frontier between the City of Edinburgh
and the Port of Leith. 'Leithers' are still fiercely proud of their independence – although
in truth they were only independent of the beady-eyed Edinburgh burgesses between 1827
and 1921. For Edinburghers found they had everything going for them, except for one
thing – a port. And so they annexed Leith and made it theirs.

Everywhere you go in Leith you are reminded of its maritime past. The Customs House
and the Mariners' Church, Baltic Street, Sand Port and Cable Wynd. Leith was the 'gateway' to
Edinburgh, and thus the gateway to Scotland. When Mary Queen of Scots returned from France
in 1561, she landed at Leith. So too her only child, James VI, in 1590 fresh from his honeymoon
in Denmark. And when George IV made his historic visit to Scotland in 1822 – the first ruling
sovereign to step on Scottish soil in 171 years – it was Leithers who welcomed him first.

Ships still come and go from the port of Leith, but the place has now
largely turned its back on the sea. Today the warehouses are occupied by designers
not dockers, the wharves frequented by fun-lovers not fishwives.

But the sea just will not go away. The royal yacht *Britannia*, pensioned off from
its ocean voyaging, has found a permanent berth not far from where another historic
royal ship, the Great Michael, was built 500 years earlier. And despite the passing of the last
Newhaven fishwife over a generation ago, somehow the smell of the briny sea, the oysters
and the mussel brose for which that fishing port was famous refuses to go away.

'They that goe down to the sea in shippes
That doe business in the great Waters
These see the works of the Lord
And his wonders in the deep'

(words from Psalm 107 inscribed on a stone at Trinity House, Leith,
built by the Fraternity of Masters and Mariners)

Old Town Rooftops and Calton Hill from the Outlook Tower

8 Collective Gallery

A contemporary visual art gallery which supports and promotes emergent artists and art forms from around Scotland, the gallery provides the opportunity to view some of the most exciting new artists in Scotland.

W2 *Cockburn Street, off Royal Mile at North Bridge.*

ᵂᶜ ♿ E FREE

⊕ All year round, Tue–Sat, 12 noon–5pm.

Tel 0131 220 1260 www.collectivegallery.net

9 Dean Gallery

A magnificent art centre situated in parkland opposite the Scottish National Gallery of Modern Art. Opened in 1999, it provides a home for Edinburgh born Eduardo Paolozzi's gift of sculpture and graphic art, including a reconstruction of his studio plus prints, drawings, plaster maquettes and moulds. Also housed here are the Gallery of Modern Art's renowned Dada and Surrealist collections, among the finest in the world, along with a superb library and archive, and a gallery fitted out as a library for the display of artists' books. The Gallery's shop contains items with a Surrealist edge, whilst Cafe Newton

is a modern take on the coffee-houses of Vienna. Temporary exhibitions change on a regular basis and can incur an admission charge; please see the website for details.

Q6 *Belford Road, W end of city.*

🅿 ᵂᶜ ♿ ✗ 🏛 E ♨ 🖼 FREE

⊕ All year round, daily, 10am–5pm.
Closed 25, 26 Dec & 1 Jan.
Entrance to permanent collection is free, but temporary exhibitions may charge entry fee.

Tel 0131 624 6200 www.natgalscot.ac.uk

10 DOM Art Centre

Edinburgh's oldest surviving house, dating from around 1480 and set in Advocate's Close off the Royal Mile, provides the venue for a range of works by living European artists. Russian paintings lie alongside British sculpture, Latvian tapestry, Spanish photography and Norwegian glasswork.

W2 *Opposite St Giles' Cathedral on Edinburgh's Royal Mile.*

ᵂᶜ 🏛 E ♨ 🖼 £

⊕ All year round, Thur–Tue, 11am–5.30pm.
Closed all day Wed.

Tel 0131 225 9271 www.artesian-arts.org

Edinburgh Castle from Johnston Terrace

11 Edinburgh Castle

Edinburgh Castle, the capital's most famous landmark, contains a wealth of interest. It houses the Stone of Destiny, the Scottish Crown Jewels (Honours of Scotland), Mons Meg, the One O'clock Gun and the National War Museum of Scotland. For more detailed information on Edinburgh Castle refer to pages 29, 30 and 31.

V2 *Top of Royal Mile, Edinburgh city centre.*

🅿 ⓦ ♿ ☕ ⌷ E ✂ £££

⏱ Apr–Sept, daily, 9.30am–6pm.
Oct–Mar, daily, 9.30am–5pm.
Last admission 45 minutes before closing.

Tel 0131 225 9846   www.historic-scotland.gov.uk

12 Edinburgh City Art Centre

The City Art Centre, which opened in 1980, has no fewer than six exhibition floors making it one of the UK's premier exhibition spaces, and the venue for a variety of temporary exhibitions from around the world. Also housed here is the city's Scottish art collection, totalling 3,500 works including paintings, photographs, tapestries and sculpture, and representing every significant influence and movement in the history of Scottish art.

X3 *Market Street, behind Waverley Station in Edinburgh city centre.*

ⓦ ♿ ☕ ⌷ E ✂

⏱ All year round, Mon–Sat, 10am–5pm.
Sun, 12 noon–5pm.
Opening times and admission both vary depending on exhibition.

Tel 0131 529 3993   www.cac.org.uk

13 Edinburgh Dungeon ★

An attraction focusing on the darker chapters in Scottish history. Visitors experience a courtroom and torture chamber, discover plague and pestilence, visit a graveyard and see Burke and Hare at work. Join the witchfinder and seek out the cannibal Sawney Bean, all via a combination of live actors, tableaux and special effects. Not for the faint-hearted.

W3 *Market Street, next to Waverley train station, Edinburgh city centre.*

ⓦ ♿ ✂ £££

⏱ Daily, Jul–Aug, 10am–7pm; Nov–Feb, 11am–4pm;
Sept–Oct & Mar–Jun, 10am–5pm.

Tel 0131 240 1000
www.thedungeons.com

EDINBURGH CASTLE

A mighty stronghold, dark and brooding atop its rocky perch, the royal castle of Edinburgh dominates its city as no other in Europe. What stories it has to tell – of bloody sieges and heroic deeds, of the births and deaths of kings, of skullduggery and base villainy. Edinburgh Castle's story is very much Scotland's story.

Man may first have stood on the castle rock during the Stone Age 8000 years ago. It was certainly a thriving hilltop settlement when the Roman legionaries marched past 2000 years ago on their way north to grapple with the Caledonian tribes. Five centuries later, King Mynyddog and his Britons rode down from their feasting hall on Din Eidyn to fight the invading Angles, the people who put the 'Eng' into England. The Britons lost, Din Eidyn was captured – and from that time on, the rock has been known by its English name, Edinburgh.

The castle rock re-emerged as a royal stronghold during the 11th century as the Scots from the north and west overran the lands of Lothian. It became the country's most important castle, serving not only as royal residence and garrison fortress but also as the home of the crown jewels – the Honours of Scotland – and the national archives. It was also the official residence of the Sheriff of Edinburghshire (Edinburgh and Midlothian).

Alas, precious little of that early castle has survived the Middle Ages; little wonder given its history. The Norman English first captured the castle in 1170. They returned with a vengeance in 1296, at the start of the bloody and prolonged Wars of Independence. Time and again, the fortress changed hands. Acts of heroism abounded, none more heroic than in April 1314 when 30 Scots, led by Robert the Bruce's nephew, scaled the precipitous north face in the dead of night and caught the English garrison off guard. They slit their enemy's throats and threw the bodies over the walls, to be dashed to pieces on the rocks below. Bruce ordered the castle's destruction, so that it would never again serve the English cause. Two months later, at Bannockburn near Stirling Castle, he sent King Edward II of England's army 'homeward to think again'.

But the castle was rebuilt, by Bruce's son, David II, and flourished under the Stewart dynasty that ruled in Scotland thereafter. Perhaps its greatest moment came in 1566 when Mary Queen of Scots gave birth there to her only child, the future King James VI of Scotland and I of England.

Mary was the last sovereign to reside in the castle. In 1573, as the rival supporters of mother and son battled it out for supremacy, a devastating artillery bombardment brought much of the east side of the stronghold crashing down. Repairs were carried out to make the castle presentable for King James's return to his birthplace in 1617, and his son, Charles I, slept the night there before his Scottish coronation in 1633. But no sooner had his head been chopped off than the man responsible, Oliver Cromwell, Lord Protector of England, captured the castle. Thereafter, the royal stronghold became little more than a garrison fortress, and into the majestic Great Hall, the chambers and chapels once the preserve of royalty, moved the military with their 'kit and caboodle'.

In 1689 the castle was besieged in earnest for the final time, as the supporters of the new Protestant sovereigns, William and Mary, succeeded in wresting the fortress from the Jacobites, the followers of the exiled Catholic James VII. Sixty years later, Bonnie Prince Charlie failed to retake the castle, and shortly afterwards the Jacobite dream was trodden into the mud at the Battle of Culloden, near Inverness.

The rediscovery by Walter Scott in 1818 of the long-lost Honours of Scotland subsequently led to Edinburgh Castle becoming a visitor attraction. Their display to the public was soon followed by the opening of King James's Birth Chamber (then in use as an arms store), St Margaret's Chapel (gunpowder magazine) and James IV's Great Hall (barrack rooms and hospital). The sound of cannons firing in earnest from the battlements was replaced in 1861 by the solitary shell of the One O'Clock Gun. Today, the ancient royal castle, built mainly to keep people out, welcomes over one million visitors each year.

Half-Moon Battery and Battlements

Look on the awesome Half-Moon Battery and you could only be in one city. There is nothing anywhere in Europe to compare with the great curved artillery wall built by Regent Morton in the aftermath of the Lang (Long) Siege of 1571-3. The impressive zig-zag ramparts on the castle's north and west sides were built after a successful breaching of the old walls by daredevil Jacobites during the '15 Rising. Ordered by General Wade, more famous for his military roads, and built by William Adam of architectural fame, the defences were never seriously tested by Bonnie Prince Charlie's troops in the '45.

Stained-glass window in St Margaret's Chapel depicting William Wallace

King Robert the Bruce Statue on the south side of the Castle Gatehouse

St Margaret's Chapel

Crowning the highest point of the castle rock, 435 ft (133m) above sea level, stands the oldest building in the castle, indeed the oldest in Edinburgh. Built around 1130 by David I in memory of his mother, St Margaret of Scotland who died in the castle in 1093, it probably originally formed part of a larger royal residence. The delightful interior, still in use for weddings and baptisms, has a fine chevron-ornamented Romanesque chancel arch and a copy of the saintly Margaret's Gospel Book.

The One O'Clock Gun

Every day, except Sundays, Good Friday and Christmas Day, at 13.00 a gun fires from Mills Mount Battery. The citizens of Edinburgh check their watches; visitors jump out of their skins. The gun was first fired in 1861, to provide an audible time signal for ships in the port of Leith. It has been fired ever since, except for periods during the two World Wars.

Mons Meg

Beside St Margaret's Chapel stands the mighty siege gun, Mons Meg – all six tons (6040 kg) of her. Forged in Mons, Belgium, in 1449, she was gifted to James II of Scotland by his uncle-by-marriage, Duke Philip of Burgundy, the richest man in Europe. Mons was carted into England more than once, but her top speed of 3 miles per day made her exorbitantly expensive, and she was soon 'retired' from active service and used as a saluting gun. In 1558, the huge 330 lb (150 kg) cannonball she fired to celebrate Mary Queen of Scots' first marriage was found 2 miles away, where the Royal Botanic Garden is today.

The Scottish National War Memorial

Scottish National War Memorial

The National War Memorial in Crown Square was built to honour the 500,000 Scotsmen killed in the Great War. It was very much the people's memorial, crafted by Scotland's finest brains and hands, and financed by public subscription. The shrine's exterior is full of symbolism – Justice is depicted blindfold with scales and a sword, Mercy as a warrior cradling a child – whilst the Hall of Honour inside sombrely details the contributions made by the twelve regiments and the other corps and services embroiled in the hideous conflict. The steel casket in the apse contains the complete Roll of Honour, and overhead soars the figure of St Michael the Archangel.

The Honours of Scotland

On display in the Crown Room are the Honours of Scotland, the oldest sovereign regalia in the British Isles. The Crown, Sceptre and Sword were first used together at the coronation of Mary Queen of Scots in 1543. Thereafter they have had the most eventful history. Following Charles II's coronation at Scone in 1651, they spent nine years buried, first at Dunnottar Castle, on the Kincardineshire coast, and then in Kinneff Church nearby. Cromwell, try as he might, failed to find them. On Charles' restoration in 1660, the Honours were returned to Edinburgh, where they represented the absent sovereign at sittings of the Parliament – until that day in January 1707 when Scotland voted for Union with the 'auld enemy' – England. For the next 111 years they remained locked away in the Crown Room until Walter Scott rediscovered them.

The Royal Apartments

In August 1617 James VI made an emotional return to the tiny room in the royal palace where he had been born 51 years earlier. The palace, little used since his departure for London in 1603, was rebuilt specially for his visit, and his Birth Chamber redecorated. Little therefore remains from his mother Mary's time, the major exceptions being the stump of the late fourteenth-century David's Tower, deep within the bowels of the Half-Moon Battery, and James IV's Great Hall, built in 1511 as the chief place of ceremony in the castle. Despite the hall's conversion into soldiers' barracks by Cromwell in 1651, and its subsequent 'restoration' in 1890, it still retains an aura of majesty.

EDINBURGH FESTIVAL, FRINGE & MILITARY TATTOO

It all began quite modestly, in a refined Edinburgh kind of way, in 1947.
It continues yet, a three-week (and more) extravaganza of music and drama, dance, exhibitions,
films – what you will – savoured by hundreds of thousands each year. The Edinburgh International
Festival has everything one could possibly wish for; as one of its former directors declared,
'it is limited only by our imagination.'
Who was to know where the opening concert that August night might lead? Rudolf Bing,
the Festival's first director, hoped it might metamorphose into an annual feast of performing arts
to rival anything elsewhere. After all, Edinburghers, Scotland and the World needed cheering
up in those cheerless days after the Second World War. They also needed bringing together,
and the determination to be truly international, not parochial, was established with that first
concert. The Orchestre des Concerts Colonne of Paris have since been joined by a glittering array
of stars journeying to Edinburgh from all over the world to amaze, and delight, and provoke.
From the start the Festival courted controversy, mostly for its perceived elitism. The world
of theatre, long renowned for its 'anti-establishmentarianism', decided to do its own thing,
and before the 'establishment' knew it, it had a rival – the 'Fringe'. Thanks to inspirational
shows such as Beyond the Fringe, first performed in 1960, the Fringe has blossomed into the
largest arts festival in the world. Today, Festival and Fringe go from strength to strength
together, as both sets of organisers would see it as friendly rivals; to you and
me – the punters – they are two sides of the same coin.
Perhaps the highlight for many is an event that began, like so many good things in life, quite
by chance. For the 1950 Festival, the Army high up in the castle decided they would like to join
in the festivities. And so they laid on a military tattoo. The simple marching and countermarching
of the pipes and drums back and forth across the Esplanade was an instant hit. Today the sight
and sound of the massed kilted bands against the dramatic backdrop of the awesome fortress
is a 'must see'. And as the sun dips in the west, and the lone piper emerges high on the
battlements to play a haunting lament, there's guaranteed to be not a dry eye in the house.

Edinburgh Castle and City from Salisbury Crags at dusk

14 Edinburgh Printmakers Workshop & Gallery

Edinburgh Printmakers Workshop an artists' studio and gallery dedicated to contemporary fine art printmaking, and the first open-access print studio in Britain. Established in 1967 by a small group of artists, including Philip Reeves, it now attracts funding from the Scottish Arts Council. The two level gallery is a thriving organisation which provides studio facilities at reasonable cost for any artists who wish to work in etching, lithography, screen printing or relief printing. Visitors can watch artists at work from the gallery viewing window and choose from a range of contemporary prints for sale.

S6 *Union Street, off the top of Leith Walk, NE of Princes Street.*

WC 🏛 E ♿ FREE

🕐 All year round,
   Tue–Sat, 10am–6pm.

Tel 0131 557 2479
www.edinburgh–printmakers.co.uk

15 Edinburgh University Collection of Historic Musical Instruments

The collections galleries, built in 1859 and still with their original showcases, are believed to be the earliest surviving purpose-built musical museum in the world and retains a Victorian atmosphere. On display are 1,000 items including stringed, woodwind, brass and percussion instruments from Britain, Europe and around the world, including many beautiful examples of the instrument-makers art over the past 400 years. Learn about the history of instruments of music via interactive devices. A new attraction is the Sound Laboratory, a hands-on approach to how musical instruments work, with live sounds, physical models, computer displays and visible effects.

X1 *Reid Concert Hall, SW corner of Bristo Square, City of Edinburgh*

WC 🏛 E FREE

🕐 All year, Wed, 3–5pm; Sat, 10am–1pm;
   Festival opening, Mon–Fri, 2–5pm;
   Closed 25/12–2/1. Groups by arrangement.

Tel 0131 650 1000   www.music.ed.ac.uk/euchmi/

16 Edinburgh Zoo

One of Europe's finest zoos, this 82 acre park is situated on leafy hillside parkland just west of the city centre, and holds over 1,000 animals, from mammals to amphibians, reptiles to birds. It is owned by the Royal Zoological Society of Scotland, and its mission is to inspire and excite visitors, thus promoting an interest in conservation. Many of the species at Edinburgh Zoo are endangered in the wild, and are held as part of national or international co-operative breeding programmes, such as the Amur tiger, red panda, Grevy's zebra, white rhino and the poison arrow frogs. All the favourites are here too – from penguins and the world's largest penguin pool, through to chimpanzees, giraffes and meerkats. Of particular popularity are the African Plains, where visitors can view the mixed zebra, oryx and ostrich species from the vantage of a long walkway into the heart of the enclosure, and the Magic Forest which is home to several species of tiny primates – marmosets and tamarins from South America. Visitors can enjoy a hilltop safari ride, with live commentary, to the top of the hill and then explore the zoo heading downhill. During the spring and summer, there are lots of additional activities such as keeper talks, close encounter animal sessions, brass rubbing and face painting. Throughout the year, there are trails for special interest groups and a full programme of themed events, talks and art exhibition.

P6 *Three miles W of Edinburgh city centre on A8.*

P ⓦ & ♿ X ⊞ E ⅍ ⊞ £££

🕐 Apr–Sept, daily, 9am–6pm; Nov–Feb, daily, 9am–4.30pm; Oct & Mar, daily, 9am–5pm.

Tel 0131 334 9171   www.edinburghzoo.org.uk

17 Fruitmarket Gallery

The Fruitmarket Gallery shows six exhibitions every year, and is renowned for its exciting and thought-provoking programme which encompasses leading national and international figures in contemporary art. The gallery is committed to maximising public involvement with its work and has developed an extensive education and events programme. Activities range from forums and lectures to workshops and outreach projects, allowing a wide range of people to access and enjoy contemporary art. In addition, visitors can relax in the street-level glass fronted cafe or browse in the bookshop.

W2 *Market Street, behind Waverley Station.*

ⓦ & ♿ ⊞ E ⊞ FREE

🕐 All year, Mon–Sat, 11am–6pm; Sun, 12 noon–5pm. Festival opening, 10am–7pm. Admission charges apply for Festival shows.

Tel 0131 225 2383   www.fruitmarket.co.uk

18 Georgian House

The Georgian House is part of Robert Adam's stylish masterpiece of urban design, Charlotte Square. It dates from 1796, when the New Town was being developed and people began to move away from the cramped and squalid conditions of the Old Town. A number of period rooms contain silver, china, paintings and furniture, reflecting the social conditions of the era. Also see entry 28 Charlotte Square (page 45).

U3 *Charlotte Square, off west end of Princes Street, Edinburgh city centre.*

⊞ E Ⓐⓥ ⊞ ££

🕐 Daily, Mar–Nov, 11am–3pm; Apr–Jun & Sep–Oct, 10am–5pm; Jul–Aug, 10am–7pm. Last admission 30 mins before closing.

Tel 0131 226 3318   www.nts.org.uk

Charlotte Square

19 Gladstone's Land

Gladstone's Land is the most important example of a 17th-century high tenement building to survive in Edinburgh's overcrowded old town. Completed in 1620, the six-storey building was originally the home of Edinburgh burgess, Thomas Gledstanes. It contains remarkable original painted ceilings, and a number of furnished rooms. A reconstructed shop booth displays replicas of 17th-century goods and the first floor of the house has been refurbished as a typical Edinburgh home of the period. See also the Georgian House (entry on page 34), a fine example of New Town architecture.

W2 *In the Lawnmarket, at the castle end of the Royal Mile.*

ff

⊕ Apr–Oct, daily, 10am–5pm; Jul–Aug, 10am–7pm.

Tel 0131 226 5856
www.nts.org.uk

20 Gorgie City Farm

Offers a wide range of both formal and informal activities focussing on farm animals, small animals (pets), horticultural, environmental and rural themes. Visitors can make use of the sensory and education gardens, and see poultry and farm animals, including piglets, calves and lambs at certain times of the year. In addition, the farm has a play area with sandpit, a workshop which produces runs and hutches, and a range of farm produce for sale.

Q5 *Gorgie Road, W end of the city.*

FREE

⊕ All year round, daily, 9am–4.30pm in the summer; 9.30am–4pm in winter.

Tel 0131 337 4202   www.gorgiecityfarm.org.uk

21 Granton Centre

The major store for the National Museums of Scotland where important conservation work is carried out and thousands of objects are prepared for display at NMS museums. The centre also plays a vital role in saving scientific evidence for research.

Q7 *West Granton Road, Edinburgh.*

£

⊕ Temporarily closed.
   Check for details of re-opening.

Tel 0131 247 4470   www.nms.ac.uk

22 Greyfriars Bobby

Lying opposite Greyfriars Kirk gates is a bronze statue of Greyfriars Bobby, a Skye terrier who famously sat by his master's grave in the churchyard for 14 years, until his own death in 1872. Bobby was 'arrested' for being unlicensed, but was reprieved by the Lord Provost and cared for by the local people, he was given the Freedom of the City. His engraved collar and feeding bowl can be seen at the Museum of Edinburgh (see page 40). John Gray's grave lies just inside the entrance to Greyfriars Kirkyard and the little dog is buried nearby.

W2 *Greyfriars Place, George IV Bridge, S of Edinburgh city centre.*

⊕ Open access

Arthur's Seat from across the Meadows

HOLYROOD PARK AND ARTHUR'S SEAT

Not many European capitals have a mountain in their midst.
Edinburgh has – Arthur's Seat, rising up from Holyrood Park to its lion-headed
summit 823 ft (251m) above. The eponymous Arthur was the legendary Dark-Age king
who is said to have bestowed on King Loth the green lands around Edinburgh that
today bear his name – Lothian. I doubt we'll ever know the
truth of the matter, or if Arthur ever did get to sit on his rocky seat.
Later legends tell also of how Holyrood got its name. David I was out hunting
one day in the royal forest of Drumsheugh when he was thrown from his horse below
Salisbury Crags and speared in the thigh by the antlers of 'a muckle white hart'.
Had it not been for the 'holy rude', or crucifix, that miraculously appeared in the king's
hands as he grappled with the stag, he would surely not have lived. But he did, and in
thanks to God David endowed a 'monastery of the Holy Rood' close to the spot of
his deliverance. That was almost 900 years ago, but the 'right of sanctuary' can still
be had within the bounds of Holyrood Park – in theory at least!
Yet there is real sanctuary to be had in the Park today, the sanctuary that
comes with peace and quiet. There, within a stone's throw (almost) of the bustling
Royal Mile, visitors and residents alike can simply relax on the grassy slopes
and beside the freshwater lochs, or explore the rocky crags teeming with
wildlife – and if you are really feeling up to it, climb
up to Arthur's Seat and take in one of the best views of any city anywhere in the world.
But once every year Holyrood Park bursts into life. Over 300 million years ago,
Arthur's Seat emerged during a violent volcanic eruption deep in the earth's crust.
The sparks that fly during Festival Sunday each August aren't by any means as spectacular
as the lava flows way back then, but you are guaranteed a cracking time.

23 Greyfriars Kirk ✝

Greyfriars Kirk was Edinburgh's first post-Reformation church, and has served the parish for nearly 400 years. Of interest are a number of impressive 19th-century stained glass windows, a 3 manual organ designed by Peter Collins, and information on the National Covenant signed here in 1638 to protest against the episcopalian form of worship introduced by Charles II. An original copy of the Covenant is on display. The church is sited in an historic churchyard which was once the garden of a Franciscan friary and now has a collection of fascinating 17th and 18th-century graves and monuments. (See City of the Dead Tours on page 24 for details on evening tours of the Kirkyard). See also Greyfriars Bobby page 35.

W2 *Greyfriars Place, off George IV Bridge, S of Edinburgh city centre.*

🚾 ♿ ♨ E 📹 FREE

🕐 Apr–Oct, Mon–Fri, 10.30am–4.30pm;
   Sat, 10.30am–2.30pm. Nov–Mar, Thur, 1.30–3.30pm.
   Services: Sun, 11am & in Gaelic at 12.30pm.

Tel 0131 226 5429   www.greyfriarskirk.com

24 Guide Friday Edinburgh Tours ★

Passengers can view Edinburgh from one of a fleet of green and cream open-top buses, and listen to commentary by a live guide. Tickets are valid all day, allowing people to leave the bus and visit attractions en route, then board again for a later tour. Each ticket also offers discounts for a number of the city's top attractions.

W3 *Tours depart from Waverley Bridge, off Princes Street, city centre. You can also join the tour at Lothian Road, Grassmarket, Royal Mile, Princes Street, George Street or the Tourist Information Centre at Princes Mall.*

🎫 £££

🕐 Buses run all year round, daily, and leave every fifteen minutes from Waverley Bridge.

Tel 0131 556 2244   www.guidefriday.com

25 Holyrood Park 🏊 🚲 🏛

This huge open area in the heart of Edinburgh contains many sites of historic interest, including a prehistoric farmstead, the remains of St Anthony's Chapel and a number

of holy wells, the most interesting of which is St Margaret's Well, a 15th-century Gothic construction. Visitors can also make use of various walks past one of three lochs, and scale Arthur's Seat, part of an old volcano offering stunning views across the city and beyond. Holyrood Lodge Information Centre houses an exhibition, and ranger service.

Z2 *E of Edinburgh city centre and SE of Holyrood Palace, on Queen's Drive.*

🅿 ♨ 🚶 FREE

🕐 Open access.
   Visitor Centre: Mon–Thur, 10am–4pm;
   Fri, 10am–3.30pm.

Tel 0131 556 1761

www.historic–scotland.gov.uk

26 John Knox House 🏰

This 16th-century medieval house belonged to the Mossman family, Mary, Queen of Scots' goldsmith/jeweller, and was believed to have been used by John Knox shortly after Mossman was declared a traitor and executed in 1573. The house has retained many of its original features such as oak panelling and a magnificent painted ceiling. An exhibition relates the stories of both Knox and Mossman, and visitors can see a display of rare books and bibles, and a reconstructed goldsmith's bench.

X2 *Around two-thirds of the way down the Royal Mile, Edinburgh city centre.*

🚾 ♿ ♨ 🎫 £

🕐 All year round, Mon–Sat, 10am–6pm.
   July & Aug, also Sun, 12 noon–6pm.

Tel 0131 556 9579

www.storytellingcentre.org.uk

MARY KING'S CLOSE

Deep beneath Edinburgh's Old Town lies Mary King's Close – a medieval street
from Auld Reekie's murky past, long since covered over and hidden from sight. Mary was
the widow of an Edinburgh merchant burgess, Alexander Nimmo. She and her four children
moved into a house at the top of the close soon after her husband's death in 1629. The street
was already known as King's Close when Mary moved in. Like other closes in the Old Town
which frequently changed their names according to the profession or name of prominent
residents, this steep alley that led off the Royal Mile down to the fetid waters of the Nor'
Loch beyond soon came to be known as Mary King's Close.

Shops and basement storerooms, inns and brothels, houses for merchants and tradesmen filled
the tenements. Low or laigh houses, often below street level, teemed with Edinburgh's poor.
These were dark, smelly, unhealthy places where large families shared single rooms with
no sanitation; every kind of waste was simply dumped in the street.

Some of the inhabitants of these old streets were struck down during the last visitation of the
plague to Edinburgh in 1645. Despite attempts to rid the town of the 'great pestilence' by
burning infected houses and quarantining the sick in their homes, perhaps as many as half of the
city's population died. It didn't take the gossips long to people Mary King's with spectres and
nameless terrors: one couple, Mr and Mrs Thomas Coulthard moved into Mary King's in 1685 but
had little chance to enjoy their new home before being haunted by the vision of an old man's
disembodied head, then by a young child, a severed arm, a dog, a cat and other weird creatures.

The Close's reputation was established and 'Those who had been foolhardy enough to peep
through the windows after nightfall saw the spectres of long-departed denizens; headless forms
danced through the moonlit apartments.' But, best known is 'Annie', a little girl who died during
the plague and whose unhappy spirit communicated with a Japanese psychic who visited the
closes in the early 1990s; since then people have been leaving gifts for the unhappy child.

The hidden closes, which form Mary King's Close, are shrouded in myth and mystery,
blood-curdling tales of ghosts and murders and of plague victims being walled up and left
to die. But now, the real stories – based on new research and archaeological evidence – are being
told and, as so often is the case, they are more fascinating than any fictional account.

27 Lauriston Castle

Lauriston began life as a 1590s tower house, and was later extended in the early 19th-century. Successive private owners enjoyed its enviable location by the Firth of Forth on the outskirts of the capital, until the estate was finally left in trust to the nation. Guided tours highlight furniture, artefacts, paintings, tapestries and porcelain, all in classic Edwardian style. In and outdoor events run from Easter to December.

P7 *Cramond Road South, NW of Edinburgh city centre.*

P WC & E ⚬ 私 ££

🕐 Apr–Oct, Sat–Thur, 11am–1pm & 2–5pm.
    Nov–Mar, weekends, 2–4pm,
    last admission 40 minutes before closing;
    Castle grounds, daily, 9.am–dusk.

Tel 0131 336 2060   www.cac.org.uk

28 Loch Ness Discovery Centre ★

A chance to learn about the environment of Loch Ness and to investigate the legend of Nessie. 3D cinema presententation in five languages with photographs, hoaxes, illusions, facts and figures, ecology, history and mystery. Suitable for all ages.

W2 *Top of the Royal Mile, Edinburgh city centre.*

WC ⊞ E AV ⊠ ££

🕐 All year, daily, April–Jun, Sept–Oct, 9am–8pm.
    Jul & Aug, 9am–10pm. Nov–Mar, 10am–5pm.
    Times may change - check for details.

Tel 0131 225 2290   www.lochnessdiscovery.com

29 Lothian Buses City Sightseeing Tours & MacTours ★

Hop on/hop off sightseeing tours of the city in open top buses with commentary on the life, architecture and scenery of Edinburgh. Mac Tours operate a vintage bus on their tours. Passengers can purchase tickets at Waverley Bridge, from the driver enroute or from Lothian Buses Travelshops.

W3 *Tours depart from Waverley Bridge.*

⚬ ⊠ £££

🕐 Frequent departures all year except
    24/25 December.

Tel 0131 555 6363
www.edinburghtour.com

30 Magdalen Chapel ✠

Built in 1541, the chapel's features make it one of the most significant churches in Scotland. Founded by Michael MacQuhane and completed by his wife after his death, it houses the only intact medieval stained glass panels in Scotland today. Tradition claims that the first General Assembly of the Reformed Kirk took place here in 1560/61. Today the Chapel is the headquarters of the Scottish Reformation Society, who are in the process of restoring the building.

W2 *41 Cowgate, Edinburgh city centre*

FREE

🕐 All year round, Mon–Fri, 9.30am–4pm.
    Other times by arrangement.

Tel 0131 220 1450

31 Mary King's Close ★

Mary King's Close lies beneath the Royal Mile. A warren of streets where people lived, worked and died. Guides will introduce you to Alexander Cant whose house was the grandest in 16th-century Edinburgh, a family of plague victims and to Andrew Chesney, 19th-century sawmaker and, of course, to the spectres and spirits. See feature on page 38.

W2 *Warriston Close, Royal Mile, Edinburgh city centre*

⊞ ⊠ £££

🕐 Apr–Oct, daily, 10am–9pm; Nov–Mar, 10am–4pm.
    Closed Christmas day.
    Children under 5 years not admitted.
    Limited disabled access-telephone for details.

Tel 08702 430160

www.realmarykingsclose.com

32 Mercat Tours ★

Guides lead walkers on a range of tours through Edinburgh's medieval Old Town and Georgian New Town. The 'Secrets of the Royal Mile' tour describes the city's great and good, while ghost tours venture down into underground vaults, originally cellars, workshops and houses, beneath the South Bridge, and include trips to an ancient tavern and historic graveyard.

W2 *Tours begin at Mercat Cross, Royal Mile, or at the Tourist Information Centre.*

WC ⊞ E ⊠ £££

🕐 All year round, day and evening tours.

Tel 0131 557 6464

www.mercattours.com

Edinburgh Castle, Princes Street Gardens and the National Gallery of Scotland

33 Museum of Childhood

The Museum of Childhood, established in 1955, was the first museum in the world to specialise in the history of childhood. Now extended to five galleries, visitors can see toys and games from the UK and beyond including a large collection of dolls, teddy bears, train sets and bicycles, and learn how children were brought up, dressed and educated in decades gone by. Temporary exhibitions and events run throughout the year.

X2 *Royal Mile, Edinburgh city centre.*

♿ ⌂ E ♿ FREE

🕐 Mon–Sat, 10am–5pm.
Sun, 12 noon–5pm.

Tel 0131 529 4142   www.cac.org.uk

34 Museum of Edinburgh

This museum, housed in 16th-century Huntly House, looks at the history of Edinburgh from pre–historic times to the present day. Exhibits include the collar and feeding bowl of Greyfriars Bobby (see page 35), Scotland's most famous dog, silver and ceramics, with a floor dedicated to Edinburgh-born Earl Haig, soldier and founder of the British Legion.

Y3 *The Canongate, Edinburgh city centre.*

♿ ⌂ E FREE

🕐 All year, Mon–Sat, 10am –5pm;
festival opening Sun, 12 noon–5pm.

Tel 0131 529 4143   www.cac.org.uk

35 Museum of Fire

The Museum of Fire tells the history of the oldest fire brigade in the UK. Housed in the historic HQ building at Lauriston, it shows the development of firefighting in an exciting and educational way. On display are a range of engines, including manual horse drawn steam and motorised pumps from 1806, along with many other fire related items from as far back as 1426.

V1 *Lauriston Place, Edinburgh*

♿ ♿ AV FREE

🕐 Mon–Fri, 9am–3pm. Closed 1–2pm.
Groups by arrangement. (Closed over Christmas & New Year; and 1st/2nd weeks of Aug).

Tel 0131 228 2401   www.lothian.fire-uk.org

36 Museum of Scotland

This striking new landmark in Edinburgh has brought together the collections of the National Museum of Antiquities and the Royal Scottish Museum, presenting the history of Scotland, its land, its people and their achievements. A series of galleries, filled with rare and precious objects, takes visitors from Scotland's geological beginnings through to the 20th-century. 'Beginnings' includes the oldest material items in the museum such as rocks and fossils formed many millions of years ago. 'Early people' looks at when people first arrived in the country and covers Norse supremacy, the Roman occupation and the introduction of Christianity. Icons of the past and objects relating to Scottish History can be found in 'The Kingdom of the Scots'. 'Scotland Transforms' illustrates Scotland's journey from a rural society to a land of cities and towns. 'Industry and Empire' looks at the influential role Scotland and the Scots have played around the world. 'Industry & Empire' brings Scotland to the end of the last millennium and the impact of life in Scotland today. Also on offer is a hands-on discovery area, and various multimedia exhibits. Interlinked with the Royal Museum, see page 55.

W2 *Chambers Street, Edinburgh city centre.*

🚾 ♿ 🍽 ✗ 🏛 E ♒ 🎫 FREE

🕐 Mon–Sat, 10am–5pm; Tue, 10am–8pm;
   Sun, 12 noon–5pm.

Tel 0131 247 4422   www.nms.ac.uk

37 National Gallery of Scotland

The National Gallery of Scotland contains a collection of paintings, drawings, prints and sculpture by great artists from the Renaissance to Post-Impressionism. Set in a handsome Neo-Classical building designed by William Playfair, it contains notable collections of works by Old Masters, Impressionists and Scottish artists. Among them are the *Bridgewater Madonna* by Raphael, Constable's *Dedham Vale* along with works by Titian, Velazquez, Van Gogh and Gaugin. The Gallery also contains the most comprehensive collection of Scottish art from the 17th-19th centuries with masterpieces by well-known figures such as Ramsay, Raeburn and Wilkie. The Gallery has undergone extensive restoration with the Royal Scottish Academy Building having been re-opened in the summer of 2003. The final stage of refurbishment has created an underground link between the National Gallery and Royal Scottish Academy buildings. The Weston Link houses a new range of facilities including an education centre, cinema, lecture theatre and information centre. Temporary exhibitions change on a regular basis, details of which can be found on the website along with a current update on the Playfair Project.

W3 *Centre of Edinburgh on the Mound, off Princes Street.*

🚾 ♿ 🍽 ✗ 🏛 E 🎫 FREE

🕐 All year, daily, 10am–5pm;
   Thur, 10am–7pm.
   Some temporary exhibitions may charge admission fee.

Tel 0131 624 6200

www.nationalgalleries.org

Moray Place

THE NEW TOWN

Edinburgh's New Town was begun more than 200 years ago, took over 100 years in the building and extended over one square mile. Its inspiration, George Drummond, the city's Lord Provost, envisioned a 'splendid and magnificent city' of broad, level streets and handsome well-ordered houses. Despite the changes wrought over time, changes that have seen Drummond's classy residential suburb metamorphose into the commercial and business heart of the modern city, Edinburgh's New Town stands today as perhaps the best example of classical town planning in Europe. It is, quite simply, 'a symphony in stone'.

For there to be a 'new' town there must have been an 'old' one. There was – Provost Drummond's own place of work and residence, the higgledy-piggledy, steep, narrow, overcrowded and unbelievably dirty wynds and closes of the medieval burgh.

Now, in the euphoria that followed the creation of the United Kingdom in 1707, Scotland's capital was to get a centre reflecting its status as Great Britain's 'second city'. Everything about the New Town proclaimed this vision. The names of the streets and squares – Hanover (the dynasty that created the United Kingdom), George (the reigning sovereign), Queen, Frederick and Princes (after Charlotte and three royal princes), Thistle and Rose (after the nations' emblems), St Andrew and St George (their respective patron saints – Queen Charlotte later insisted that her name replace England's saint). Even the original plan (it was subsequently altered) proposed by the 22-year-old James Craig, winner of the design competition in 1766, resembled

Moray Place and Ainslie Place

Heriot Row

the Union Jack – one central square with the streets radiating off it!
The Mound, linking the 'new' to the 'old', began as a short-cut in 1781, enabling George Boyd's New Town customers to continue to patronise his tailoring premises in the Old Town; whence its nickname – Geordie Boyd's Brig.

The New Town wasn't intended for any old 'Tom, Dick or Harry'; it was to be an aristocratic suburb, the preserve of 'people of fortune and a certain rank'. In the event most never took up the invitation. In their place came the business and professional classes from the Old Town. As the 'magnificent city' rose up, and its graceful crescents spread north and west down to the Water of Leith and east towards Calton Hill, so the Old Town, emptied of its classier residents, spiralled further into squalor and decline.

Today, both towns happily co-exist. Together they are the heart of a great metropolitan city, each contributing its own unique blend of buildings and spaces to create the World Heritage Site that is Edinburgh Old and New Town.

38 National Library of Scotland 🏛

The National Library of Scotland grew out of the Advocate's Library, founded for the legal profession in the late 17th-century. This treasure house contains books, manuscripts, music and maps, especially relating to Scotland and the Scots, with reading rooms open for reference and research only. During the summer visitors can enjoy exhibitions on a variety of Scottish historical and literary themes.

W2 *George IV Bridge, Edinburgh city centre*

ᵂᶜ ⅙ 🦽 ♿ E ♿ FREE

🕐 Exhibtion Hall, June-October,
   Mon-Fri, 10am-5pm;
   Festival 10am-8pm; Sat, 10am-5pm;
   Sun, 2-5pm.

Tel 0131 226 4531   www.nls.uk

Nelson Monument, Calton Hill

39 National War Museum 🏛

The National War Museum, (formerly the Scottish United Services Museum), is situated in 18th-century buildings within Edinburgh Castle, and explores the Scottish experience of war and military service over the last 400 years. Each gallery looks at a different theme, ie. 'A Nation in Arms' looks at how strategy and military service have influenced Scottish history, while 'A Grand Life for a Scotsman' explores the individual's experience of military life, from recruitment through to retirement. Other sections focus on weapons, equipment and clothing; the story of the Highland soldier; how the civilian population dealt with military service in home defence and war; and personal experiences by those in active service.

V2 *Within Edinburgh Castle, top of the Royal Mile, Edinburgh city centre. Admission charge is included in admission to enter Edinburgh Castle.*

🅿 ᵂᶜ ⅙ 🦽 ✗ 🏛 ☀ E ♿

🕐 Apr–Oct, daily, 9.45am–5.45pm.
   Nov–Mar, closes 4.45pm.

Tel 0131 225 7534   www.nms.ac.uk

40 Nelson Monument ★

Erected in the early 19th-century, this upturned telescopic-shaped tower honours Admiral Nelson's victory and death at the Battle of Trafalgar. Visitors can climb to the top of this 100ft tower and enjoy views across the city. A time ball, added in 1852, is lowered every day (except Sunday) as the One O'Clock gun is fired from Edinburgh Castle, and every year, on October 21, Trafalgar is marked by a special flag display.

X3 *East end of Edinburgh city centre, on Calton Hill.*

🅿 ☀ £

🕐 Apr–Sept, Mon, 1–6pm; Tue–Sat, 10am–6pm.
   Oct–Mar, Mon–Sat, 10am–3pm.

Tel 0131 556 2716   www.cac.org.uk

41 Newhaven Heritage Museum 🏛

Set in an historic fish market on the banks of the Firth of Forth, Newhaven Heritage Museum tells the story of the once thriving fishing community which was based in the village of Newhaven. Reconstructed sets of fishwives and fisherman, historic objects and photographs, and personal experiences come together to form a fascinating picture of a unique way of life based around sea fishing.

R8 *Pier Place, Newhaven Harbour, N of city centre.*

P & ⌂ E AV FREE

⊕ All year, daily, 12 noon–4.45 pm.

Tel 0131 551 4165   www.cac.org.uk

42 No. 28 Charlotte Square   ⌂

Charlotte Square was the last commission by influential architect Robert Adam (1728-92), and is regarded as one of the finest Georgian squares in Britain. In 1996, the National Trust for Scotland bought No.'s 26-31 with the hope of initiating a renaissance of the square. The houses now act as the head office of the Trust, and contain a Drawing Room Gallery, gift shop, coffee house and restaurant. On display in the gallery room is a collection of 20th-century Scottish paintings, including works by Scottish Colourists, and a number of fine pieces of Regency furniture. Also of note in Charlotte Square is the Georgian House (see entry on page 34).

U3 *Edinburgh city centre, off west end of Princes Street.*

WC & ☕ ✗ ⌂ E £ FREE

⊕ Open 6 Jan–24 Dec.
   Drawing Room Gallery: Mon–Fri, 11am–3pm.
   Shop & Coffee House: Mon–Sat, 9.30am–5pm.
   Restaurant at No. 27: Tue–Sat, from 6pm.

Tel 0131 243 9300   www.nts.org.uk

43 Our Dynamic Earth ★

This unique attraction, nestled under Arthur's Seat, uses the latest technology to tell the history of planet Earth. Visitors travel back in time to witness the Big Bang from the deck of a spaceship, see the formation of the earth, and go on to experience volcanoes, earthquakes, glaciers, polar ice and a tropical rainstorm. Special events such as exhibitions, activities, workshops and lectures, run throughout the year. Please telephone or see website for details.

Y2 *Bottom of Holyrood Road, Edinburgh, next to the Palace of Holyroodhouse and opposite the new Scottish Parliament.*

P WC & ☕ ⌂ E AV ☀ £ £££

⊕ Apr–Oct, daily, 10am–5pm.
   Nov–Mar, Wed–Sun, 10am–5pm.
   Last entry 80 minutes before closing.

Tel 0131 550 7800   www.dynamicearth.co.uk

44 The Outlook Tower, Camera ★
Obscura and World of Illusions

An attraction, dating from the 19th-century, at which live panoramic views of the city are projected on to a large screen, and a guide entertains with stories of Edinburgh's past. Free telescopes give views of 360 degrees towards Edinburgh Castle and across the whole city. A permanent gallery looks at the art and science of holography, while the 'Edinburgh Vision' section allows visitors to interact with various images of the city, old and new, and stand inside a giant pinhole camera. A 'Magic Gallery' contains 200 years of visual trickery with hands-on exhibits.

W2 *Adjacent to the castle, Royal Mile, Edinburgh city centre.*

WC ⌂ E AV ☀ £ £££

⊕ Apr–Jun & Sept–Oct, daily, 9.30am–6pm.
   Nov–Mar, daily, 10am–5pm. Jul–Aug, daily,
   9.30am–7.30pm.
   Last presentation 1 hour before closing.

Tel 0131 226 3709   www.camera–obscura.co.uk

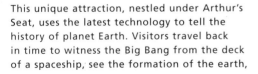

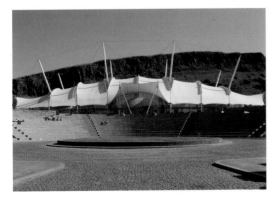

THE OLD TOWN

Edinburgh's medieval 'Old Town' was a city of contrasts – of broad market places and narrow wynds, at once 'picturesque' and 'odorous', a capital city claustrophobically constrained within its tight defensive wall, its inhabitants left with nowhere to go but up, up into the sky – which they did to perfection; the 'great tenement' behind Parliament Square was fourteen storeys high.

Walking down the Royal Mile today, from castle to palace, one can be forgiven for thinking it was always one historic town. In fact, it was two towns 'joined at the hip', the royal burgh of Edinburgh growing up under the protection of the king in his castle, and Canongate ('the Canons' Way'), established by the Augustinian canons of Holyrood Abbey. Stand at the junction of High Street and Canongate and you stand where the two once met – confronted each other would be more apt, for the rivalry between the two neighbours continued almost unabated right down to 1856 when they merged to help create the modern City of Edinburgh. Edinburgh was always the more powerful neighbour. Trade was its life-blood, and there were markets everywhere – a fish market, flesh (meat) market, lawn market and grass market. You name it, they sold it – except lawns and grass of course; the Lawnmarket and Grassmarket were so named from the quality of the goods on sale, the former specialising in fine items such as cloth, the latter in basic household wares, like the candles made in nearby Candlemaker Row.

The Old Town was truly cosmopolitan, a city where the high-born and the low-life rubbed shoulders. For the first 400 years, the inhabitants clung to the narrow rocky spine sloping down from castle and abbey. But when Edinburgh became 'de facto' the capital of Scotland around 1500 and the population spiralled upwards, the great aristocratic families moved to new townhouses in the town of Canongate, whilst the wealthiest merchants relocated to pastures new outside the city wall.

The Cowgate Burn to the south became the 'in' place to live, and soon the green valley was graced with fine houses. But in their wake followed the growing populace, and so the wealthy moved again, onward and outward – to George Square, the New Town and so on. The city is expanding yet, but its ancient heart remains, nine centuries old and still going strong.

The Old Town still retains its magic, that sense of wonderment, for resident and visitor alike. Sir Walter Scott, born in College Wynd (where Guthrie Street is today), a stone's throw away from the Mercat Cross, called it 'mine own romantic town'. That says it all.

Looking towards the Pentland Hills across the Old Town and the domed McEwan Hall

THE PALACE OF HOLYROODHOUSE

At the foot of the Royal Mile stands the imposing Palace of Holyroodhouse, the official residence in Scotland of the British royal family. For one week in July, 'royal week', pomp and pageantry return once more to the ancient 'house of Kings' as the sovereign and court take up residence therein. Military bands parade, people flock to the Palace Grounds for the annual Garden Party, and carriages constantly come and go, conveying their royal occupants to official engagements the length and breadth of the land. It was not always so. Although the history of Holyrood reaches back almost 900 years, its first residents weren't kings but Augustinian canons. It was they who built the great abbey of the Holy Rood ('holy cross') on their arrival in 1128, and they who founded the town of Canongate in its shadow. It was they too who, as the years went by, made the royal family welcome in their guesthouse during their stays in Edinburgh; the castle, 'that windy and right unpleasant spot', made a great fortress but a poor residence.

As Edinburgh grew in importance, so the royal family chose to reside at the abbey more often. By the time of the Reformation in 1560 they had made the abbey their principal home, converting the ancient medieval guesthouse into a modern renaissance palace. The national spotlight now shone upon the Palace of Holyroodhouse as James V and his French queen, Marie of Guise, their daughter Mary Queen of Scots, and

her son James VI of Scotland and I of England, strutted and sparkled on the international stage. The Palace of Holyroodhouse became 'Caledonia's Palace of Versailles'.

But one dark deed perpetrated therein blots out all the palace's pomp and pageantry – the brutal murder of Mary's confidante, David Rizzio, during a supper-party in her royal apartment one evening in March 1566; the Italian clung to his queen's skirts as the knife blows rained down on him. The dagger of Mary's second husband, the dastardly Darnley, was later found near the bloody scene. The chamber where the deed took place is there yet, though the blood-stains have gone long since. But much of what the visitor admires today dates from the time of Mary's great-grandson, Charles II, who around 1670 ordered that the Palace be rebuilt as the official residence of his viceroy, the Secretary for Scotland. The old royal apartment in the north-west corner was reserved for the sovereign's use, but in the event it was never required. Neither Charles II nor his successors bothered to visit their northern kingdom, and by the time George IV came, in 1822, after a royal absence lasting 200 years, Holyrood was in such a state that the king preferred to reside at Dalkeith Palace, seven miles away, using the Palace only for formal receptions. Only after Queen Victoria purchased the Balmoral estate in 1848 did the Palace of Holyroodhouse become once more Scotland's 'house of Kings'.

The Palace of Holyroodhouse – Northwest Tower

45 Palace of Holyroodhouse 🏰 ✠
& Holyrood Abbey

Situated at the foot of Arthur's Seat and
in the pleasant surroundings of Queen's Park,
the palace is the official residence of Her
Majesty the Queen in Scotland. Visitors
can see an impressive array of furnishings,
plasterwork ceilings and tapestries in the
State Apartments. The remains of Holyrood
Abbey, located within the grounds, date
back to the 12th and 13th-centuries.
The Queen's Gallery, newly opened in 2002,
exhibits fine art from the Royal Collection.
See special feature page 49.

Z3 *At the E end of the Royal Mile, Edinburgh
city centre.*

🚻 ♿ ♨ 🖼 £££

🕐 Apr–Oct, 9.30am–5pm. Nov–Mar, 9.30am–3.30pm.
Last admission 1 hour before closing.
Times subject to change at short notice.

Tel 0131 556 7371
www.theroyalcollection.org.uk

46 Parish Church of ✠
St Cuthbert

St Cuthbert, the 7th-century Border shepherd
who became a monk, is reputed to have pitched
his tent in the sheltered hollow below Edinburgh
Castle rock. The present church, completed in
1894, is the seventh religious building on this
oldest ecclesiastical site in Edinburgh. Features
of interest include the 18th-century steeple,
fine marble decoration in the chancel and
one of the few genuine Tiffany windows
in Scotland. Visitors can also see an early
19th-century watchtower where a nightly
vigil was kept to protect the graves from
bodysnatchers. Among the notable people
buried in the churchyard are John Napier,
inventor of logarithms and the decimal point,
writer Thomas de Quincey, painter Alexander
Naysmith, and George Meikle Kemp, designer
of the Scott Monument.

V2 *West end of Princes Street Gardens,
with entrances also on Lothian Road, Princes Street
and King's Stables Road.*

🅿 🚻 ♿ ☕ ♨ E 🌿 FREE

🕐 Visitor Centre: Mid Apr–Mid Sept,
Mon–Sat, 10am–4pm.

Tel 0131 229 1142
www.st-cuthberts.net

47 People's Story 🏛

Located in the 16th-century Canongate
Tolbooth, the museum recounts the story
of the people of Edinburgh from the end
of the 18th-century to the present day.
A series of reconstructions which include
a prison cell, cooper's workshop, a 1940's
kitchen, washhouse, pub and tea room
are accompanied by sights, sounds and smells
of the city's past. These reconstructions are
accompanied by collections of photographs,
everyday objects and rare artifacts plus
video presentation.

Y3 *Next to Canongate Church, near the foot
of the Royal Mile.*

🚻 ♿ ♨ E AV FREE

🕐 All year round, Mon–Sat, 10am–5pm;
Festival opening, Sun, 2–5pm.

Tel 0131 529 4057
www.cac.org.uk

48 Prestonfield Golf Course 🚩18

Prestonfield Golf Club is set in parkland
below Arthurs Seat, bound by Holyrood
Park and Duddinston Loch. The Club
was established in 1920 and the present
layout is by James Braid. Its reputation
of being a challenging but fair course
has made it a popular venue for a number
of competitions over the years.

S5 *Holyrood Park, two miles S of Edinburgh
city centre*

🅿 🚻 ♨ ✕ 🖼 £££

🕐 Telephone to book.

Tel 0131 667 9665
www.prestonfieldgolfclub.com

Princes Street at dusk

51

PRINCES STREET & GARDENS

It was intended as the eye-catching frontispiece to Edinburgh's New Town,
'the magnificent city' of Provost Drummond's dreams. In the event Princes Street never
quite lived up to expectations, failing to attract the 'right sort' of resident, and ultimately
playing 'second fiddle' to George Street and the elegant squares to either end. Nevertheless,
the highway once regarded as the most beautiful in Europe has survived the vicissitudes
of time, and the vagaries of town-planners, to remain a real pleasure to walk along and
from which to admire the ancient castle and the 'ridgy back' of the Old Town.
An Edinburgh silk merchant by the name of Neale was the first to build on Princes Street,
in 1769. Others followed, but reluctantly and only after inducements were offered by the
City Fathers. Perhaps Princes Street was too uncomfortably close to the Nor' Loch for
would-be residents; once noted for its fine trout and tasty eels, by the eighteenth
century it had become little more than the town rubbish dump,
the haunt of 'worried cats and drowned dogs'.
Princes Street should have been called St Giles Street, but George III, who had never
been to Scotland and wasn't aware that Giles was Edinburgh's patron saint, would have
none of it; he thought that it referred to a seedy run-down 'slum' in London!
Instead it was named after the two royal princes of George III and Queen
Charlotte – the Duke of Rothesay (the future George IV) and the Duke of York.
Gradually, though, the residents did come, not quite the class of people originally envisaged,
but well-to-do merchants intending to take full advantage of their new situation.
They built their houses, and they laid out their gardens on the site of the drained Nor' Loch.
Through Victoria's long reign, whilst the other New Town streets retained their residential
charm, Princes Street became the focus for commerce, sprouting businessmen's premises,
gentlemen's clubs, giant department stores and grand hotels, what Robert Louis Stevenson
called 'a terrace of palaces'. Even the private gardens were abandoned by their owners
and turned into public pleasure grounds. And that's what you'll find there today.

49 Princes Street Gardens ❋

Princes Street Gardens lie in the centre of Edinburgh below the castle walls and along the length of Princes Street. occupying the valley between the Old Town and Princes Street. The gardens now flourish where the Nor' Loch, a defensive artificial loch, was created in 1460. Over time the loch became the Old Town's rubbish dump, polluted by the butchers and tanners who worked on its banks. Originally designed as private gardens for the New Town residents; they were finally opened to the general public in 1876. Found within the gardens are the famous Floral Clock, Ross Fountain and Ross bandstand, which hosts musical concerts and other events in the summer months.

V3 *Princes Street, Edinburgh city centre*

wc ♿ FREE

🕒 Open all year, dawn to dusk.
Check with TIC for summer programme.

Tel 0131 225 6844

50 Royal Botanic Gardens ❋
Edinburgh

Set in over 28 hectares of beautifully landscaped grounds, plant collections from around the world, from the tender to exotic, to those native to Scotland, flourish. Established in 1670 as a physic garden in Holyrood, the gardens are an internationally renowned centre for scientific research, horticulture, conservation and education. The gardens consist of the Heath Garden, which recreates plantings and landscapes found naturally in the Scottish Highlands, the neighbouring Rock garden is home to over 5000 alpine plants. The Chinese Hillside garden shows of the historical links the garden has with China where familiar plants can be seen, many of which were collected during the late 19th and early 20th centuries. The Glasshouse Experience includes Britain's tallest Palm House and leads you on a journey through the tropical and temperate regions of the world. The gardens also offer panoramic views of the city skyline and provide a programme of events, exhibition, activities and an art galley.

R7 *Inverleith Row, one mile N of city centre.*

wc ♿ 🐕 ✕ 🏛 E ☘ 👥 ♨ FREE

🕒 Open daily from 10am; Closes: Apr–Sept, 7pm; Mar & Oct, 6pm; Nov–Feb, 4pm.
Closed 25 Dec & 1 Jan. Admission charges applies to Glasshouse. Guided tours run from Apr–Sept.

Tel 0131 552 7171

www.rbge.org.uk

51 Royal Burgess Golf ▶18
Course

This inland course of 6,494 yards and par 71 was founded in 1895. One of its main features is the positioning of many mature trees. The classic layout of the course can be attributed to alterations in the late 1940s by James Braid. Visitors to Royal Burgess will enjoy a day's golf on well manicured fairways and greens only a short distance from Edinburgh's City Centre.

O7 *Off A902 Queensferry Road at Barnton roundabout, W of the city centre.*

P wc 🏛 ✕ ♨ £££

🕒 Telephone to book.

0131 339 2075

www.royalburgess.co.uk

52 Royal College of 🏛
Surgeons Museum

The museum houses both the Sir Jules Thorn Exhibition of the History of Surgery and the Menzies Campbell Dental Museum. Displays illustrate the scope of modern surgery and include examples of surgical specialities. The exhibition also describes the history of surgery and Edinburgh's special contribution to surgical practice from ancient to modern times. The Dental Museum is one of the the largest dental collections in the country and demonstrates the development of dentistry from its early days to modern times.

X2 *Second floor at the Royal College of Surgeons, 9 Hill Square, a few minutes walk S of North Bridge.*

wc E FREE

🕒 All year round, Mon–Fri, 12 noon–4pm, except Diploma days & public holidays

Tel 0131 527 1649

www.rcsed.ac.uk

The Royal Mile and St Giles' Cathedral from the Outlook Tower

53 The Royal Mile ★

Running from the Castle to the Palace of Holyroodhouse, is Edinburgh's most famous street. At almost a mile long it runs from east to west taking in Castlehill, the Lawnmarket, the High Street and Canongate. The early buildings which fronted the street, grew upwards as the Old Town expanded, creating the tenements and alleyways or closes which charactises the Royal Mile, many of which were named after their former occupants. Today there is a wealth of history to explore along with attractions, museums, shops, restaurants and cafes. During the Edinburgh Festival, the High Street is awash with colour as artistes and street performers promote their events at the festival. See special feature on page 56 for more information.

X2   *Royal Mile, Edinburgh city centre.*

FREE

☺ Open access to the street.
   Please check times for individual attractions, shops etc.

54 Royal Museum 🏛

This elegant Victorian building with its beautiful glass-topped roof contains outstanding collections of decorative arts, science, industry, archaeology and the natural world. The natural history galleries focus on a huge range of animal life, along with evolution, gems, rocks, minerals and fossils. Other highlights include a section on Ancient Egypt, the art and design of the Middle East, China, Japan and Korea. Examples of European and Classical glass, ceramics, ironwork, arms and armour are on show, while the Western Decorative gallery exhibits a fine array of contemporary arts dating from 1850. The European Arts section features six centuries of sculpture, silver, ceramics, tapestries and furniture. Interlinked with the Museum of Scotland, see page 41.

W2   *Chambers Street, Edinburgh city centre.*

wc & ♥ 🏛 E ♿ FREE

☺ Mon–Sat, 10am–5pm;
   Tue, 10am–8pm;
   Sun, 12 noon–5pm.
Tel 0131 247 4219
www.nms.ac.uk

55 Royal Observatory Visitor Centre 🏛

Set on Blackford Hill in beautiful 19th-century historic buildings, the Observatory rooftop offers panoramic views across Edinburgh. The 'Reach for the Stars' section relates the history of the Royal Observatory and Astronomy in Edinburgh, while the 'Discovery Zone' contains hands-on exhibits on the subject of light. Also on offer is one of the largest telescopes in Scotland, and a computer gallery which gives information on the wonders of the universe. Winter lectures, public observing (Oct–Mar) and astronomy classes run at various times, and events and workshops are organised for school holidays.

R5   *Leave City Bypass at Straiton Junction, follow A701 to lights at West Mains Road, turn left, follow signs.*

🅿 wc 🏛 E ☀ 🚶 ♿ ££

☺ Fri only, 7–9pm.
   Booking essential check website for further details.
Tel 0131 668 8405   www.roe.ac.uk

56 Royal Yacht Britannia ★

The royal yacht *Britannia*, launched at Clydebank in 1953, served the Royal Family for over forty years, and travelled over a million miles. Now berthed at Leith, visitors can take a self–led audio tour of five decks (children's handsets are available), and discover what life was like for the royals, officers and yachtsmen on board. On show is the royal dining room, sitting room and sun lounge on the verandah deck, along with the bridge and engine room. As well as the vessel itself, visitors can tour the visitor centre which houses an audio-visual presentation, the royal barge, reconstructed wheelhouse and an exhibition of photographs featuring the royals on the *Britannia*. Following *Britannia's* move to Ocean Terminal at the end of 2001, further areas of the ship have been opened for visitors including the Royal Marines barracks, the laundry and the sick bay.

S8   *Berthed at Ocean Terminal. Signposted through Leith, NW end of Edinburgh; a dedicated bus runs from Waverley Bridge, beside Waverley train station.*

🅿 wc & 🏛 E ♿ £££

☺ Mar–Oct, daily, 9.30am–4.30pm (closes 6pm).
   Nov–Feb, daily, 10am–3.30pm (closes 5pm).
   Closed Christmas & New Year's Day.
Tel 0131 555 5566   www.royalyachtbritannia.co.uk

THE ROYAL MILE

There are many fine city streets in the world, but there is nothing quite like the Royal Mile. Castlehill, Lawnmarket, High Street, Canongate and Abbey Strand link arms to form the historic roadway uniting the great royal castle at its head to the imposing royal abbey and palace at its foot. From the outset in the twelfth century, kings and queens have travelled up and down the cobbled causeway between the two centres of power - one thinks of Mary Queen of Scots making her way from palace to castle in 1566 for the birth of her only son, the future King James VI of Scotland and I of England; of James's own son, Charles I, riding out from the castle for his coronation in Holyrood Abbey in 1633; and most recently of Her Majesty Queen Elizabeth progressing up the Royal Mile in the State Coach for the official opening of Scotland's new Parliament in 1999. The *via regis*, the Royal Mile, is still very much at the heart of Edinburgh's, and Scotland's, public life, an observation that becomes readily apparent as you walk down it. At the junction of Castlehill and Lawnmarket stands the Tolbooth Kirk, built for the General Assembly of the Church of Scotland in the 1840s. Even as it was being constructed, the national church splintered into two, and the newly-formed Free Church of Scotland audaciously built its rival Assembly Hall directly opposite, on the other side of Castlehill. The former is now 'the Hub', the centre around which the Edinburgh International Festival weaves its magic; the latter served as the temporary home of the new Scottish Parliament. Where Lawnmarket and High Street meet stands the High Kirk of St Giles. This much-altered twelfth-century edifice

was the medieval city's only parish church until Charles I converted it into a cathedral in 1633 and had its Presbyterian congregation decanted to a new church, the Tron Kirk, further down the Royal Mile. Even though the High Kirk housed a bishop's throne for just 33 of its 800 years of life, it is still popularly known as 'St Giles' Cathedral'. Behind St Giles, tucked away in a labyrinth of later buildings, lies Scotland's old Parliament Hall. The first debate took place in 1639, the last in 1707 when the members voted for political Union with England and themselves out of a job; since then, the Hall has served as the seat of the Court of Session, the supreme court of Scotland. Prior to 1639, Parliament met in the Tolbooth, a building that served the needs of both city and state, including most ghoulishly as the chief place of execution. Known affectionately as 'the Heart of Midlothian', it was demolished 200 years ago, but if you look down at the cobbles near the west door of St Giles you'll see a 'heart' marking where it once stood. On the east side of St Giles is the Mercat Cross, a Victorian recreation of the original. If St Giles was the soul of the city, the Mercat Cross was its throbbing heart. Alas, so central was it to Old Town life that it got in the way of traffic and was pulled down in 1756. The plan was that the Cross would be replaced by the Royal Exchange (the building directly across from St Giles now serving as the City Chambers). It housed a custom house, coffee houses, shops and dwellings all under one roof. But the merchants much preferred to 'wheel and deal' where they'd always done, out in the open around the Mercat Cross. So in 1811 the City Fathers took

Ramsay Garden

Castlehill

Lawnmarket

Wardrop's Court and Lady Stair's Close

Canongate

White Horse Close

over the redundant Exchange for their own use, demolishing their previous home, the rickety old Tolbooth, in the process. Where High Street meets Canongate was the point where the towns of Edinburgh and Canongate met. Canongate was always the poor relation. Only in the sixteenth century, when the later Stewart sovereigns held court at Holyrood, did Canongate rival its neighbour. Hints of that former glory still remain in the lower reaches of the Royal Mile – the fine Tolbooth, where its own Town Council met, the starkly impressive Canongate Kirk, built in 1688 for the Presbyterian congregation displaced by James VII from Holyrood Abbey, and those once-grand townhouses of ancient aristocratic families who danced attendance on their sovereign in the nearby palace.

One of those townhouses, Queensberry House, erstwhile residence of the first Earl of Lauderdale, is shortly to re-emerge in a new guise, for it forms part of the new home of the Scottish Parliament now rising from the ground at the foot of the Royal Mile. When the Parliament building opened in 2004, the old town of Canongate, for so long in Edinburgh's shadow, assumed an importance in the life of the nation it has not experienced since those halcyon days of James V and Mary Queen of Scots.

The Royal Mile was very much the public face of the 'Old Town', but behind the affluent facades was where the real life of the city was lived, in the crowded closes and dark wynds leading off the ridge to north and south. One observer likened the Royal Mile and its side streets to 'a guttit haddie [gutted haddock], its myriad bones laid bare'. Each of those 'bones' has a tale to tell, perhaps a dark secret to give up, none more so perhaps than Brodie's Close, off the Lawnmarket, where Deacon Brodie lived; burgess by day but burglar by night, he became the inspiration for Robert Louis Stevenson's 'Dr Jekyll and Mr Hyde'. The Royal Mile might not be quite a mile long, but 'every inch of it is historical'.

THE SCOTT MONUMENT

He was born in College Wynd, in Edinburgh's
Old Town in 1771; he passed away 60 years later
at his beloved Abbotsford, in the rolling Border
hills 30 miles to the south. In between, the literary
'colossus' penned 26 'blockbusters', hundreds
of poems and thousands of letters. These 'scribblings'
are his real monument. But the monumental pinnacle
towering over Princes Street, raised by his fellow
countrymen and women, ensures that this creative
genius will never be forgotten by those living in,
and visiting, the city.

The statistics of the Scott Monument are as
prodigious as Scott's literary output. 200 ft (61m)
high, 287 steps winding up to that breathtaking view,
64 statues of his favourite characters, and at its heart
the seated man himself with his faithful deerhound,
Maida, by his side, carved from a single block of
Carrara marble – all 30 tons of it.

Scott would have approved of the choice of architect,
for George Meikle Kemp was the son of a Border
shepherd. Border blood coursed through Scott's veins,
and following his move to Selkirkshire on his
appointment as its sheriff-depute in 1799, he spent
many happy hours in their company, wrapped in
wonderment at their stories and ballads. His masterful
Minstrelsy of the Scottish Border sits alongside
his own compositions in the Scott legacy.

But Scott never forgot Edinburgh, 'mine own
romantic town'. He purchased a house in fashionable
Castle Street (no.39), in the emerging New Town,
and there he wrote many of his epics, among them
The Heart of Midlothian, centred on the grim
and massive tolbooth in the heart of the Old Town.
"Antique in form", he described it, "calculated
to impress all beholders." Scott could have been
describing his own Monument.

57 Russell Collection of Early Keyboard Instruments

The Russell Collection of Early Keyboard
Instruments, housed at St Cecilia's Hall is one of
the world's most important collections of its type
and presently comprises of over 50 instruments
dating from the end of the 16th-century to the
beginning of the 19th-century. Instrument types
include the harpischord, spinet, virginal,
clavichord, organ and fortepiano.

X2 *St Cecilia's Hall, Niddry Street, Edinburgh city centre.*

   E FREE

⊕ Wed & Sat, 2pm-5pm. Closed Christmas & New Year.

Tel 0131 650 2805   www.music.ed.ac.uk/russell

58 Scotch Whisky Heritage Centre

The Scotch Whisky Heritage Centre, beside
Edinburgh Castle, reveals the history, mystery
and romance of Scotch whisky making.
Visitors can learn how the 'water of life'
is produced, and discover from a tour guide,
the subtle differences between whiskies
from the Highlands, Lowlands, Speyside
and the islands. The resident ghost makes
an appearance, and a barrel ride runs through
the history of Scotch whisky. The bar at the
Whisky Barrel Restaurant provides a selection
of over 270 single malts, blends and liqueurs,
and serves a range of whisky cocktails, while

the shop offers rare and unusual malts and blends, plus a variety of miniatures.

W2 *Top of the Royal Mile, adjacent to Edinburgh Castle.*

🚻 ♿ ♥ ✕ ☖ AV ⊞ £££

🕐 All year round, daily, summer, 9.30am–5.30pm; winter, 10am–5pm. Closed Christmas Day.

Tel 0131 220 0441
www.whisky–heritage.co.uk

59 Scott Monument ★

Following the death of writer Sir Walter Scott in 1832, an architectural competition was launched welcoming designs for a suitable memorial. The winner was George Meikle Kemp, and his imposing 200 ft monument was erected in the city centre between 1840 and 1846. Features include carvings of Scott's literary characters and a statue of the writer himself made from marble. Visitors can still climb the 287 steps to the top and admire panoramic views over Edinburgh. See feature on page 58.

W3 *East Princes Street Gardens, by Princes Street, Edinburgh city centre.*

E ⚘ £

🕐 Apr–Sept, Mon–Sat, 9am–6pm; Sun, 10am–6pm. Oct–Mar, Mon–Sat, 9am–3pm; Sun, 10am–3pm.

Tel 0131 529 4068   www.cac.org.uk

60 Scottish Genealogy Society ★

The Library and Family History Centre contains a wealth of material for the genealogist. Founded in 1953, the Society has amassed a diverse and fascinating collection of books and manuscripts covering many subjects, from reference books to individual family collections. There is also a large and expanding collection of microfiche, microfilm and CDs ranging from Mormon and census collections to old parish records, which can be viewed in the library. Volunteer members of the Society will answer general queries from the library resources.

W2 *Victoria Terrace, Edinburgh city centre.*

🚻 ☖ ⊞ FREE

🕐 Mon, Tue and Thur, 10.30am–5.30pm; Wed, 10.30am–8.30pm; Sat, 10am–5pm; Closed Fri.

Tel 0131 220 3677   www.scotsgenealogy.com

61 Scottish National Gallery of Modern Art 🏛

The Scottish National Gallery of Modern Art houses Scotland's finest collection of 20th and 21st-century paintings, sculpture and graphic art. The collection is specifically western art, with works by artists such as Matisse, Picasso and Dali. The gallery also holds a fine collection of 20th-century Scottish art including paintings by Bellany, Gillies, Peploe, Davie and Redpath. The gallery buildings are situated in extensive parkland, providing the perfect setting for sculptures by Henry Moore, Barbara Hepworth and Anthony Caro among others. Temporary exhibitions change on a regular basis, details of which can be found on the website.

Q6 *Belford Road, in the W end of Edinburgh.*

🅿 🚻 ♿ ♥ ☖ E ⚘ 👥 ⊞ FREE

🕐 All year, daily, 10am–5pm; Closed 25/26 Dec. Entry to the permanent collection is free, but there may be an admission for temporary exhibitions.

Tel 0131 624 6200   www.natgalscot.ac.uk

62 Scottish National Portrait Gallery 🏛

The Scottish National Portrait Gallery provides a unique visual history of Scotland told through portraits of figures who shaped it, including royals and rebels, poets and philosophers, heroes and villains. All the portraits are of Scots, but not all are by Scots, with works by great English, European and American masters such as Van Dyck, Gainsborough, Rodin and Kokoschka, along with Ramsay, Raeburn and other Scottish artists. Sculptures, miniatures, coins, medallions, drawings and watercolours and also housed here, along with the National Photography Collection. For details on the changing programme of temporary exhibitions, please see the website.

W3 *E end of Queen Street, near St Andrew Square, Edinburgh city centre.*

🚻 ♿ ♥ ☖ E ⊞ FREE

🕐 All year daily, 10am–5pm; Thurs until 7pm. Closed 25/26 Dec. Entry is free, but there may be a charge for temporary exhibitions.

Tel 0131 624 6200   www.natgalscot.ac.uk

63 Scottish Parliament ★

Visitors can see Parliament in action in the new Scottish Parliament building opened in September 2004. An exhibition explains the workings and history of the Scottish Parliament along with self-guided tours. On business days you can arrange to observe a committee or a full meeting of the Parliament in progress (booking advised). You can also watch proceedings on screens in the Main Hall. In depth guided tours, lasting approximately 45 minutes, are available on non-business days (charge applies), see website for further details. Public information staff are available to answer visitor's questions. Access to the building is free.

Y3 *Holyrood, at the foot of the Royal Mile.*

🚻 ♿ 🚼 ☖ E 🅿

🕐 Business days (normally Tues-Thur), all year, 9am–7pm.
Non-business days (normally Mon & Fri and every weekday when in recess): Apr–Oct, 10am–6pm; Nov–Mar, 10am–4pm.
Weekends, all year, 10am–4pm.
Closed 25/26 Dec & 1/2 Jan.

Tel 0131 348 5200   www.scottish.parliament.uk

64 Scottish Poetry Library 🏛

The Scottish Poetry Library founded in 1984 and housed in a brand new building, has an unusual collection on written works, tapes and videos. The emphasis is on Scottish contemporary poetry in Scots, Gaelic and English. Scottish historical works along with contemporary works from other parts of the world are also featured. Visitors have access to resources, advice and information.

Y3 *Crichton's Close, Canongate, Edinburgh city centre*

🚻 ♿ ☖ E 🅿 FREE

🕐 Mon–Fri, 11am–6pm; Sat, 1–4pm.
Closed 1st & 3rd Mon in May; 3rd Mon in Sept & 24 Dec–3 Jan.

0131 557 2876   www.spl.org.uk

65 Scottish Rugby Murrayfield Stadium Tours ★

Feel the passion of Scottish Rugby for yourself by taking a behind the scenes tour of Murrayfield Stadium. Follow in the footsteps of legends as you visit the dressing rooms, players tunnel, Royal Box, hospitality suites, the press gallery and the world famous pitch. Tours last about 1hour 15 minutes. Bookings must be made 48 hours in advance.

Q6 *Roseburn Street, W of Edinburgh city centre.*

🚻 ♿ ☖ E 🆎 ££

🕐 Tours: Mon–Fri at 11am & 2.30pm.
Weekends and bank holidays by arrangement.

Tel: 0131 346 5000   www.scottishrugby.org

66 Spirit of the Tattoo Visitor Centre ★

Located in the shadow of Edinburgh Castle, Spirit of the Tattoo tells the story of the Edinburgh Military tattoo experience through an interactive exhibition.

W2 *Top of the Royal Mile, Edinburgh city centre.*

🚻 ♿ 🍽 ✕ ☖ E 🆎 🍴 🅿 FREE

🕐 Summer: Mon–Sat, 10am–5pm. Sun, 11am–5pm.

Tel 0131 225 9661
www.edinburgh-tattoo.co.uk

67 St Giles' Cathedral ♧

Known as the 'Cradle of Presbyterianism', St Giles' Cathedral, located in the heart of Edinburgh's Old Town, has been a centre of intrigue, bloody history and fascinating legend for over 1000 years. Evidence suggests that a church stood on this site as far back as the 9th-century, but the current building was erected in the 14th and 15th-centuries. External features include its unique crown spire, an integral part of the city's skyline for the last 500 years. Inside, visitors can see memorials to many great Scots such as Stevenson and Burns, modern and traditional stained glass windows and Lorimer's early 20th-century Thistle Chapel with its famous bagpipe playing angel. For information on free guided tours and lunchtime summer concerts, please telephone the number below or see the website.

W2 *Parliament Square, on the Royal Mile, Edinburgh city centre.*

🚻 ✕ ☖ 🍴 🅿 FREE

🕐 May–Sept, Mon–Fri, 9am–7pm; Sat, 9am–5pm.
Oct–Apr, Mon–Sat, 9am–5pm;
Sun, all year, 1–5pm.

Tel 0131 225 9442   www.stgiles.net

St Giles' Cathedral, High Street, Royal Mile

Deacon Brodie's Tavern, Lawnmarket

68 St Mary's Episcopal Cathedral ✠

This Victorian Gothic Cathedral was completed in 1879 to the award-winning design of Sir George Gilbert Scott and is the largest ecclesiastical building to be built in Scotland since the Reformation. Of particular note are the pelican lectern, Lorimer's rood, the high altar screen featuring the Scottish saints, Columba and Margaret and the new stained glass windows, designed by Sir Eduardo Paolozzi, in the south transept.

R6 *Palmerston Place, W end of Edinburgh city centre.*

♿ ⊞ FREE

🕐 All year round, daily, 7.15am–6pm; Summer, closes at 9pm. Daily services held.

Tel 0131 225 6293   www.cathedral.net

69 Tartan Weaving Mill and Exhibition 🏛

Visitors can experience the atmosphere of a real working tartan mill and learn how tartan cloth is made, from shearing sheep to spinning, dyeing and weaving. They can try their hand at weaving on a hand pedestal operated loom; dress up in a plaid and have their photograph taken. At the information centre visitors can discover and research their own clan and tartan history from the archives.

W2 *Top of the Royal Mile, adjacent to Edinburgh Castle, Edinburgh city centre.*

♿ 🍴 ✗ ⊞ E ♿ ££

🕐 Apr–Oct, daily, 9am–6.30pm; Nov–Mar, closes at 5.30pm;

Tel 0131 226 1555
www.tartanweavingmill.co.uk

70 The Hub Festival Centre ★

This historic building, the former Highland Tolbooth, with Edinburgh's most dominant spire, has been fully restored and is now the year round focus for cultural life and hub of the Festival City. Information on the Festival along with concerts, lectures, workshops, exhibitions and education projects.

W2 *Castlehill, Royal Mile, Edinburgh city centre.*

WC ☕ ♿ 🎫 FREE

🕐 All year, Tue–Sat, from 9.30am, closing times vary.
Sun–Mon, 9.30am–6pm.
31 Dec, 9.30am–6pm. Closed Christmas Day.

Tel 0131 473 2000 www.eif.co.uk

71 Tron Old Town Information & Visitor Attraction ★

Inside the Tron Kirk is the Old Town Information Centre along with the lost street of Marlin's Wynd demolished in 1635 to make way for the new church and discovered in 1974.

X2 *Tron Kirk, Royal Mile, Edinburgh city centre.*

♿ ♿ E FREE

🕐 All year round. Apr–Oct, daily, 10am–5pm.
Nov–Mar, daily, 12 noon–4pm.

Tel 0131 225 8408

72 University of Edinburgh Centre 🏛

The University of Edinburgh was founded in 1583 by Royal Charter and, with funding from the town council, became established a year later as the 'Tounis College'. Since then, the life of the university has been intertwined with that of the city and is associated with characters both distinguished and notorious. The university's history involves a royal murder, the infamous Deacon Brodie and Burke & Hare as well as more revered figures such as David Hume, Charles Darwin, Joseph Black, Robert Louis Stevenson, Sir Walter Scott, Sir Arthur Conan Doyle and Winston Churchill. Many of the university's buildings are amongst the city's most famous landmarks – none more so than Old College with its distinctive dome and quadrangle. This was designed by Robert Adam and completed after his death by the young William Playfair, who designed most of the interiors and lends his name to the Playfair Library Hall. Originally a working library, it is now used for ceremonial purposes and lectures – an impressive venue with a magnificent barrel vaulted ceiling and fluted Ionic pillars. Old College houses art collections and exhibitions in the Talbot Rice Gallery and the Raeburn Room, which takes its name from the fine collection of portraits it contains by Sir Henry Raeburn.

X2 *On the corner of Chambers Street and South Bridge. Tours commence from the University Centre on Nicolson Street, next to the Old College.*

WC ♿ ♿ E £

🕐 Guided tours given at 1pm on the last Fri of each month and regularly throughout Aug (please check for details).
Talbot Rice Gallery: Tue–Sat, 10am–5pm.

Tel 0131 650 2252 www.ed.ac.uk

73 Water of Leith

The Water of Leith is a narrow river that runs from the Pentland Hills, through the heart of the city and eventually empties into the Firth of Forth at Leith. Walkers can follow the river via a number of scenic pathways. A visitor centre looks at life on the water via interactives, an exhibition and video.

Q5 *Visitor centre: SW of city centre, Lanark Road, Slateford.*

P WC ♿ ☕ ♿ E AV ⛷ 🚶 ££

🕐 Walkways: open access.
Visitor Centre: Apr–Sept, daily, 10am–4pm.
Oct–Mar, Wed–Sun, 10am–4pm.

Tel 0131 455 7367 www.wateroflleith.edin.org

74 Writers' Museum 🏛

Scotland's three great writers, Sir Walter Scott, Robert Louis Stevenson and Robert Burns, are honoured in the historic 17th-century Lady Stair's House. A collection of portraits, manuscripts and exhibits of personal items include Burns's writing desk, Scott's chessboard and the printing press on which the *Waverley Novels* were produced. Other Scottish writers feature in a programme of changing exhibitions.

W2 *Below Edinburgh Castle on the Royal Mile, Edinburgh.*

WC ♿ E FREE

🕐 All year round, Mon–Sat, 10am–5pm; Festival opening, Sun, 12 noon–5pm. Times may change, please telephone or check website for details.

Tel 0131 529 4901 www.cac.org.uk

Dean Village – originally called 'Water of Leith Village'

WATER OF LEITH, DEAN VILLAGE & STOCKBRIDGE

'Edinburgh's powerhouse' or 'a great open ditch for receiving every kind of filth' - take your pick; both descriptions of Edinburgh's main river held good two centuries ago. Emerging from the Pentland Hills to the south of the city, and twisting through 20 miles before entering the Forth at the port of Leith, the 'Great Water of Leith' was Edinburgh's jugular vein from the time of its foundation in the twelfth century through to the day when the steam-engine finally replaced water-power a century and more ago. As the great Scots engineer, Thomas Telford, oversaw the building of his elegant Dean Bridge in 1830, some 80 mills had joined the 'mills at the Dene' set up in the gorge below in the 1140s by the canons of Holyrood Abbey. Their names live on still - in Canonmills, Silvermills and so on.

The gushing waters of the Great Water powered all sorts of machinery, including 'pungent tanneries and blacksmiths' shops melodious with the clank of the anvil'. But mostly they powered grain mills. Over a doorway into Baxters' Granary, down Bell's Brae in the Dean Village, is an inscription: GOD BLESS THE BAXTERS OF EDINBRUGH UHO BULT THIS HOUS 1675. Two hundred years later the Baxters Incorporation ('baxter' is Scots for 'baker') moved to better, larger premises in Leith, and the Dean Village went into decline.

But the topsy-turvy eccentricities of the Dean Village have come to its aid in recent times, and today the quaint informality of the place offers welcome relief from the classical neatness of the New Town above. Robert Louis Stevenson wrote of 'that dirty Water of Leith', made so by the raw sewage pouring into it from the New Town; some of it, of course, from his own house at 17 Heriot Row!

The Forth Bridges from the air

AROUND EDINBURGH

'the heavy-laden grainfields'

The green lands of Lothian fringing Edinburgh, the poet Hugh MacDiarmid's 'heavy-laden grainfields', are framed to the north by the salt-waters of the Forth and on the remaining three sides by the gently rolling Southern Upland hills – the Bathgates, Pentlands, Moorfoots and Lammermuirs. Legend has it that King Loth held sway here 1500 years ago, ruling from the impressive hillfort of Traprain Law, in East Lothian. But Loth's native Britons, having recently seen off the Romans, were soon overrun by other invaders – the pagan Angles sweeping up from the south around AD 600. They in turn were ousted by the Gaelic-speaking Scots from the north and west.

The presence of Loth and his successors lives on today in towns and villages across the region; the Welsh-speaking Britons have left us Bathgate (*baedd coed* 'boar wood') and Penicuik (*pen y gog* 'hill of the cuckoo'), Angles called Hadda and Leving settled down at Haddington and Livingston, whilst we have the Gaels to thank for Auchendinny (*ach an-t Sionnaigh* 'field of the fox') and Balerno (*baile airneach* 'settlement of the sloe trees'). But it is Hadda and Leving's language we now speak, or a form of it; Welsh and Gaelic have come and gone.

After 1100, Lothian was divided into three shires, each under the control of a sheriff – Linlithgowshire, Edinburghshire-and-Haddingtonshire; a singularly uninspired bureaucrat changed them to West, Mid and East Lothian in the nineteenth century. Farming predominated then, as well as fishing in the coastal waters out of ports from Blackness to Dunbar. Today the fishing boats have all but gone, though working the 'heavy-laden grainfields' still remains the preoccupation of many. But even agriculture has given ground in recent centuries to other pre-occupations. Coal, first discovered by the monks of Newbattle a thousand years ago, transformed the landscape around Dalkeith and Tranent during the Industrial Revolution, whilst shale did the same for West Lothian, once James 'Paraffin' Young's scientific and entrepreneurial skills had created the world's first oil industry in 1850.

The coal and shale bings are largely gone now from the green lands. New industries have taken their place, most crucially the 'sunrise' factories centred on the new town of Livingston, part of Scotland's 'Silicon Glen'. Leisure and tourism have also ridden to the rescue. Today, visitors can enjoy 'the gowf' over East Lothian's fine links courses, stroll and boat along the 200-year-old Union Canal through the douce West Lothian countryside, and even see what it was like to be a coal-miner at the Lady Victoria Colliery Museum in Newtongrange. You can even call in on King Loth at Traprain Law – though I doubt you'll find him in.

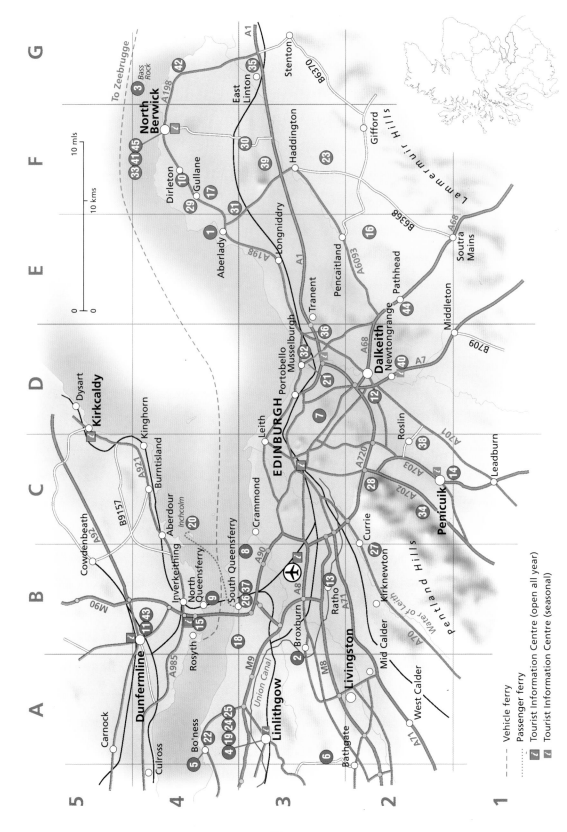

ATTRACTIONS AROUND EDINBURGH

1 Aberlady Bay Nature Reserve

Aberlady Bay Nature Reserve made up of mudflats and saltmarshes is a haven for birds with over 250 species visiting the area annually. Declared a reserve in 1952, it is now designated as a Grade 1 Site of Special Scientific Interest. With well defined footpaths and trails, the access from the car park is via a bridge and boardwalk.

E4 *Off A198, 6 miles SW of North Berwick*

🅿 🌿 👫 FREE

🕙 Open access

www.aberlady.org

2 Almondell and Calderwood Country Park

A scenic and tranquil park composed of two estates along the River Almond. Facilities include walks, barbecue area and a ranger service.

B3 *Two miles S of Broxburn; turning signposted off A89 at Broxburn*

🅿 🚻 ♿ 🍴 🎠 🏕 🌿 👫 FREE

🕙 Daily, Summer, 9am–5pm. Winter, 10am–4pm.

Tel 01506 882254

3 Bass Rock

Located off the coast of North Berwick in the Firth of Forth, it measures one mile in length, with sheer cliffs dropping down at all sides. Signs of human life include a lighthouse, and ruins of a 16th-century chapel, a castle and prison, but the rock is best known as a bird sanctuary, attracting thousands of gannets every year. Visitors can sail round the island on organised boat trips. See also the Scottish Seabird Centre page 80.

G4 *The Bass Rock is three miles off the coast of North Berwick. Boat trips on the Sula II leave from North Berwick harbour.*

🌿 ££

🕙 Daily trips run during summer months, weather permitting.
Contact operator for timetable.

Tel 01620 892838 (boat operator)

4 Beecraigs Country Park

A country park set in the Bathgate Hills above Linlithgow, offering a range of activities including walking, riding and cycling routes, park centre, play area and ranger service.

A3 *Two miles S of Linlithgow, close to J3 & 4 off M9*

🅿 🚻 ♿ ✗ 🎠 🏕 🌿 👫 🎫 FREE

🕙 Daily, throughout the year, times vary

Tel 01506 844516

www.beecraigs.com

The Bass Rock, Firth of Forth

5 Bo'ness & Kinneil Railway and Birkhill Fireclay Mine

The Scottish Railway Exhibition tells the story of the development of railways and their impact on the Scottish People. Historic railway buildings, including a station and train shed, have been relocated from sites all over Scotland. A train journey takes passengers into the West Lothian countryside to Birkhill, where guided tours lead into the underground workings of Birkhill Fireclay Mine, with its ancient fossils.

A4 *Bo'ness eight miles W of the Forth Road Bridge.*

P ᵂᶜ ♿ ✕ 🏛 E ⛩ 🧗 💷 ££

🕐 Apr–Oct, Sat–Sun, 11am–5pm.
Jul–Aug, Tue–Sun, 11am–5pm.
Last entry 4pm.

Tel 01506 825855   www.srps.org.uk

6 Cairnpapple Hill

This important archaeological site was used for burial and ceremonial purposes from around 3000-1400 BC. Visitors can see burial areas, ancient stones and a cairn, situated in an area with stunning views towards Arran and the Trossachs.

A3 *Off A706, three miles N of Bathgate.*

P 🏛 E 🌿 £

🕐 Apr–Sept, daily, 9.30am–6.30pm.

Tel 01506 634622
www.historic–scotland.gov.uk

7 Craigmillar Castle

This L-plan tower house ruin was expanded in the 15th and 16th-centuries, and is very well preserved. Mary, Queen of Scots stayed in the castle after the murder of her secretary, David Rizzio, at Holyroodhouse.

D3 *Three miles SE of Edinburgh, off the A68.*

P ᵂᶜ ♿ ☕ 🏛 E £

🕐 Apr–Sept, daily, 9.30am–6.30pm.
Oct–Mar, Sat–Wed, 9.30am–4.30pm
(closed Thur and Fri).

Tel 0131 661 4445
www.historic–scotland.gov.uk

Dirleton Castle, East Lothian

8 Dalmeny House

Dalmeny, the home of the Earls of Rosebery for over 300 years, contains fine 18th-century French furniture, tapestries, porcelain, and portraits by Gainsborough, Raeburn, Lawrence and Reynolds. The house also holds an impressive Napoleonic collection.

B3 *On Firth of Forth, eight miles W of Edinburgh city centre; turn off A90 to B924, Dalmeny/South Queensferry exit.*

P WC ☕ ££

⊕ Jul–Aug, Sun–Tue, 2–5.30pm
   (last admission 4.30pm).

Tel 0131 331 1888   www.dalmeny.co.uk

9 Deep Sea World

Scotland's national aquarium contains one of Europe's largest collections of sand tiger sharks and an underwater safari tunnel, where divers can be seen during daily feeding sessions. Other exhibits include ruins from the volcanic eruption of Krakatoa with submerged temples and statues, the flooded forest of the Amazon with piranhas, stingrays and electric eels, and a display of amphibians. Various fish feeds and presentations take place during the day.

B4 *North Queensferry; take J1 off M90 and follow signs.*

P WC & ☕ ✕ 🏛 E AV 🎁 £££

⊕ All year round, daily.
   Hours vary according to time of year;
   please ring or see website for details.
   An annual pass allows unlimited admission
   for a year.

Tel 01383 411880
or 24–hour information line 0906 941 0077
(calls cost 10p per minute)
www.deepseaworld.com

10 Dirleton Castle

Originally built in the 13th century, Dirleton was captured by the English in 1298, subsequently regained by Robert the Bruce in 1311 incurring severe damage. Rebuilt in the 14th and 16th-centuries, when its gardens were first recorded, which now include the world's longest herbaceous border.

F4 *Dirleton, three miles W of North Berwick on the A198.*

P & 🏛 E £

⊕ Apr–Sept, daily, 9.30am–6.30pm.
   Oct–Mar, daily, 9.30am–4.30pm.

Tel 01620 850330
www.historic–scotland.gov.uk

11 Dunfermline Palace & Abbey

The site marks the remains of a Benedictine abbey founded by Queen Margaret in the 11th-century. Robert the Bruce was buried in the nave, now the site of the present parish church. Next to the abbey is the ruin of the Royal Palace, birthplace of Charles I, the last monarch born in Scotland.

B4 *St Margaret Street, Dunfermline, off the A907*

🏛 E £

⊕ Apr–Sept, daily, 9.30am–6.30pm;
   Oct–Mar, Mon–Sat, 9.30am–4.30pm
   (closed Thur afternoons and Fri)
   Sun, 2–4.30pm

Tel 01383 739026
www.historic–scotland.gov.uk

EAST LOTHIAN GOLF COURSES

10,000 years ago, the last ice cubes melted away and the land beneath, breathing a huge sigh of relief, rose up out of the rising seas. Over 9,000 years later, man took to hitting a wooden ball with a wooden stick over the raised beaches left behind by the receding ice – and the rest is history. The Scots may not be able to prove they invented golf, but they certainly perfected it and gave it to the world. And East Lothian's challenging links courses, stretching along the sandy coastal fringe all the way from Musselburgh to Dunbar, have more than played their part.

'The gowf' may have been played over the undulating grassy tufts at Musselburgh for centuries before the first 'medal' was played for in 1774. When the Honourable Company of Edinburgh Golfers, the world's oldest golf club, moved from its original home in Leith to the bracing links beside the River Esk in 1836, Musselburgh became the 'Mecca' of golf. A gentleman called Mungo Park won the first 'Open' held there in 1874; six more followed in quick succession.

But then in 1891 the Honourable Company took its mashie niblicks and feathery balls along the coast to Muirfield. Musselburgh's loss was Muirfield's gain, and the sandy dunes beside the pretty village of Gullane have been its home ever since. Muirfield's first 'Open' was played over 72 holes in the following year, and in 2002 the course hosted its twelfth, when Ernie Els carried off the coveted silverware.

Today there are golf courses all across the county, ranging from traditional links to parkland courses and providing a range of challenges to suit every need, from the professional to the humble 'hacker'. Even the kids are catered for, with their very own course behind the Marine Hotel in North Berwick. The game has come a long way since James II decried the pastime in 1447 and attempted to ban it. He should have known better.

12 Edinburgh Butterfly and Insect World ★

Visitors can wander through a large indoor tropical rainforest with waterfalls and pools and observe the natural behaviour of hundreds of free-flying birds and butterflies. There are also daily handling sessions of snakes, spiders, giant centipedes and stick insects in a 'Bugs and Beasties' section. A display of a leaf-cutter ant colony and a variety of poisonous frogs, scorpions and insects are also on show.

D2 *Off Edinburgh city bypass at Gilmerton exit or Sheriffhall Roundabout.*

P WC & 🦽 ✗ 🏛 E 🎋 🎎 ♿ ££

🕑 Summer, daily, 9.30am–5.30pm.
  Winter, daily, 10am–5pm.

Tel 0131 663 4932
www.edinburgh–butterfly–world.co.uk

FORTH RAIL BRIDGE

On 4 March 1890 a steam train chugged across the Forth Rail Bridge, from Lothian
to Fife. The privileged passengers on board included the Prince of Wales, who moments
before had officially opened the forest of steel spanning the Queensferry Narrows a little
up-river from Edinburgh. Already, John Fowler and Benjamin Baker's huge structure was being
hailed as 'the eighth wonder of the world'. Another of the passengers on that chilly morning,
Gustave Eiffel, designer of the equally famous Tower by the Seine, can only have
acknowledged the engineering brilliance of his British counterparts.
Yet it could all have gone disastrously wrong. No sooner had the Forth Railway Bridge Company
appointed their first-choice engineer, Thomas Bouch, than his previous creation crumpled into
the murky waters of the River Tay, 40 miles to the north, during a violent storm; 75 souls
perished. Fearing a repeat, Bouch was instantly dismissed – and what should have been a great
suspension bridge metamorphosed into Fowler and Baker's elegant cantilevers of steel.
The simple statistics are staggering enough – 1.5 miles (2.5km) long; 340 ft (104m) high
at its highest point; 55,000 tons of steel; 8,000,000 rivets (the last one driven home by the
Prince of Wales himself); 640,000 cu ft of Aberdeen granite; 62,000 cu ft of other stone.
Sadly, there is another statistic. Thirty-six men fell to their deaths, and another
461 were seriously injured, during the eight years it took William Arroll Engineers to
build the bridge. Sixty-three people died producing Scotland's industrial miracle of the
nineteenth century. Think of them next time you sit in your railway carriage
staring out bewitched through Baker and Fowler's great achievement.

13 Edinburgh Canal Centre ★

The centre is set in landscaped gardens alongside the Union Canal, which was opened in 1822 and originally constructed to transport coal into Edinburgh; it now acts as a venue for a range of cruises and events.

B3 *Ratho, near Edinburgh Airport, between the M8 and A71. Follow signs for Ratho from Newbridge Interchange or Dalmahoy Golf & Country Club.*

P WC & ✗ ☀ 🕴 ♿

⏱ Cruise times vary. Bridge Inn: all year round, Mon–Thur, 12 noon–11pm; Fri–Sat, 12 noon–midnight; Sun, 12.30–11pm.

Tel 0131 333 1320/1251
www.bridgeinn.com

14 Edinburgh Crystal Heritage Centre ★

A heritage centre tells the story of glassmaking in Scotland and the history of Edinburgh Crystal. A demonstration area allows visitors to see the craftsmen at work transforming plain crystal into the finished pieces with glass cutting and engraving taking place. Visits are self-guided. Many beautiful and unusual pieces are on display along with museum pieces, artefacts, videos and show cases.

C2 *Take A701 from Edinburgh City Bypass, travelling S to Penicuik.*

P WC & 👜 ✗ ☖ E 🎏 ♿ FREE

⏱ All year round, Mon–Sat, 10am–5pm; Sun, 11am–5pm.

Tel 01968 675128
www.edinburgh–crystal.com

15 Forth Bridges Exhibition 🏛

Drawings, models, artefacts and a video tell the history of the unique road and rail bridges spanning the Firth of Forth; visitors can admire views towards the bridges and across to the opposite shoreline.

B4 *Queensferry Lodge Hotel, N of Inverkeithing; on B981 off A90*

P WC & 👜 ✗ ☖ E 📺 ☀ ♿ FREE

⏱ All year round, daily, 9am–9pm

Tel 01383 417759
www.forthbridges.org.uk

16 Glenkinchie Distillery 🍺

A working distillery established in 1837, visitors can see the distillers at work, producing a classic lowland malt using water from the nearby Lammermuir Hills. Features an exhibition, guided tour and tastings.

E2 *At Peaston Bank, turn S off A6093 at Pencaitland.*

P WC & ☖ E 📺 📏 🕴 ♿ ££

⏱ Easter–Oct, Mon–Sat, 10am–4pm (last tour); Sun, 12 noon–4pm. Restricted hours in winter; telephone for details.

Tel 01875 342004   www.malts.com

17 Gullane Golf Course ⛳

Gullane has been an important centre for the game of golf since it was established in 1882. Gullane No1, the principal of the three courses here, has been a venue for many important championships in its long history. This is a links course of 6,466 yards with a par of 72, and has panoramic views over the Firth of Forth.

F4 *On A198, 16 miles E of Edinburgh*

P WC & ✗ ☖ ☀ ♿ £££

⏱ Booking essential

Tel 01620 842255
www.gullanegolfclub.com

18 Hopetoun House 🏰

Home of the Marquis of Linlithgow, Hopetoun House is situated in extensive parkland by the Firth of Forth, with views of the famous bridges and the Fife coast. Hopetoun is really two houses in one. The oldest part, built between 1699 and 1707, was designed by Sir William Bruce and contains fine examples of carving, wainscoting and ceiling painting. In 1721, William Adam started enlarging the house and added a facade and State Apartments which were to become the focus for social life and entertainment in the 18th-century. Visitors can study the rooms, and admire the opulent gilding and classical motifs, along with fine furniture, paintings, tapestries and ceramics. The parkland, which extends

Hopetoun House – west face

to 100 acres, includes a deer park and an ever-changing carpet of seasonal flowers.

B4 *South Queensferry, 12 miles NW of Edinburgh city centre.*

P WC 🅿 ♿ ⛟ 🏛 🎋 🧗 🎫 £££

🕐 Apr–Sept, daily, 10am–5.30pm; Last entry one hour before closing.

Tel 0131 331 2451
www.hopetounhouse.com

19 House of the Binns

Situated in extensive parkland, this 17th-century house has been the home of the Dalyell family for nearly 400 years, and reflects the transition in Scottish architecture from fortified stronghold to more spacious mansion. Visitors can see impressive moulded plaster ceilings along with a collection of late 18th and 19th-century furnishings, a run of family portraits and an interesting selection of china. The surrounding grounds feature a woodland walk which leads to a panoramic viewpoint across the Firth of Forth, with displays of snowdrops and daffodils in spring.

A3 *Linlithgow, fifteen miles W of Edinburgh on A904.*

P ♿ 🎋 🧗 🎫 ££

🕐 House: June–Sept, Sat–Thur, 2–5pm.
Parkland: Apr–Oct, daily, 10am–7pm;
Nov–Mar, daily, 10am–4pm.

Tel: 01506 834255   www.nts.org.uk

20 Inchcolm Abbey and Island

The well-preserved ruins of an Augustinian monastery, founded c1123, lie on the island sanctuary of Inchcolm in the Firth of Forth, the centuries old retreat of St Colm. But today's tranquillity belies its turbulent past. When the wars in the Middle Ages with the English were at their height, the Augustinian canons often had to abandon the monastery to escape the English pirates and during the First World War, Inchcolm was used to help defend the Forth from German Zeppelins. Today the abbey ruins include an octagonal chapter house and cloister of the 13th/14th-centuries. The island's wildlife include seals, dolphins, puffins, various other sea and shore birds. Access is via the Maid of the Forth ferry, which takes passengers under the century old Forth Rail Bridge.

C4 *Inchcolm, Firth of Firth. Ferry service from Hawes Pier, South Queensferry, and Town Pier, North Queensferry.*

WC ♿ 🏛 E 🎋 £££

🕐 Apr–Oct, weather permitting; timetable ferry service (telephone for details). Cruise takes 3 hours with 1.5 hours on the island.

Abbey: Tel 01383 823332
www.historic-scotland.gov.uk
Cruises: Tel 0131 331 5000
www.maidoftheforth.co.uk

21 Inveresk Lodge Garden

This terraced garden in the historic village of Inveresk entices visitors with its colourful herbaceous beds, a variety of attractive shrubs, and a collection of old roses selected by Graham Stuart Thomas. The Edwardian conservatory contains an aviary, tree ferns and hardy exotics, while many of the plants in the informal area hold the royal Horticultural Society's Award of Garden Merit. The hillside part of the garden provides views of the Pentlands.

D3 *Six miles E of Edinburgh city centre at Inveresk, on A6124, S of Musselburgh.*

& WC £

All year, daily, 10am–6pm or dusk if earlier.
House not open to the public.

Tel 01721 722502   www.nts.org.uk

22 Kinneil Museum

Housing local history exhibits, including the story of the estate since Roman times, the 17th century stable block also acts as an interpretative centre for the Kinneil Estate.

A4 *On the S shore of the Firth of Forth W of Edinburgh on A904.*

P WC E AV FREE

All year, Mon–Sat, 12.30–4pm.

Tel 01506 778530   www.falkirk.gov.uk

23 Lennoxlove House

Lennoxlove, the family seat of the Duke of Hamilton, is set in 460 acres of woodland in the heart of East Lothian. The house is believed to date back to the 15th-century, and was initially known as Lethington Tower. Visitors can see a number of rooms, including the barrel-vaulted Great Hall, chapel and dungeon, and admire fine examples of interior design work by renowned Scottish architect Sir Robert Lorimer. Furniture, paintings, and the death mask and silver casket of Mary, Queen of Scots are among the other highlights. The grounds feature woodland walks, a sunken lawn, herbaceous borders and sculpted landscape.

F3 *Two miles S of Haddington, off B6368/9.*

P WC & E £££

Closed for major refurbishment during 2006. Re-opening 2007.
Telephone or check website for details.

Tel 01620 823720
www.lennoxlove.org

24 Linlithgow Canal Centre

Linlithgow is on the Edinburgh & Glasgow Union Canal which stretches for 32 miles (50 km), and, when built in 1822, linked the centre of Edinburgh to the Forth & Clyde Canal at Falkirk. The Linlithgow Union Canal Society voluntary group run a centre here, offering boat trips to the Avon Aqueduct (two-and-a-half hours) on the St. Magdalen, a forty-seater canal boat, and shorter trips on the Victoria (30 minutes). A small museum contains photographs and canal artefacts.

A3 *Manse Road Basin, Linlithgow; follow signs.*

WC & E AV ££

Easter–Sept, weekends, 2–5pm.
Jul & Aug, daily, 2–5pm.
Trips: Easter–Sept, weekends from 2pm.
Wheelchair access to museum, toilets and tearoom only. Museum entry is free.

Tel 01506 671215   www.lucs.org.uk

25 Linlithgow Palace

Built in the 15th-century, Linlithgow has many connections with royalty, being a popular residence of the Stewart kings and queens; it was the birthplace of James V and Mary, Queen of Scots, and Bonnie Prince Charlie spent a night here in 1745. The impressive ruins are set in parkland by Linlithgow Loch which has a large population of wildfowl. See feature opposite.

A3 *Linlithgow, off the M9 at J3 northbound; J4 southbound.*

P WC E £

Apr–Sept, daily, 9.30am–6.30pm.
Oct–Mar, daily, 9.30am–4.30pm.

Tel 01506 842896
www.historic–scotland.gov.uk

26 Maid of the Forth

Enjoy views of the Forth Bridges as you cruise downriver to Inchcolm Island. On board commentary tells you of the features and sealife as they pass, see seals and possibly dolphins and porpoises and a variety of seabirds. Telephone or check the website for details of cruises available.

B3 *Curises depart from Hawes Pier, (under Forth Rail Bridge) South Queensferry.*

& £££

Regular sailings, weather permitting.
Call for details or visit the website.

Tel 0131 331 5000   www.maidoftheforth.co.uk

LINLITHGOW PALACE

Eighteen miles west of Edinburgh, along the road to Stirling, lies Linlithgow.
You'll find the pace of life in West Lothian's pretty county town very different
from that in the capital city. It has long been thus.
In medieval times Scotland's kings and queens found Linlithgow not only convenient for the main
power centres of Edinburgh and Stirling, but more importantly sufficiently removed from those
political cauldrons to enable them to relax. So there, on a grassy knoll beside the little loch
(Linlithgow may derive from *llyn llaith cau* 'wet hollow lake'), they built a fine manor house.
Nothing now remains of the original residence, built by David I in the early twelfth century,
for it was destroyed in a great fire that swept through the town in 1424. But James I,
of the royal house of Stewart, turned tragedy into triumph and built a beautiful stone
palace in its stead. And that is what the visitor admires today.
The Stewarts loved Linlithgow Palace. There they could enjoy themselves – feasting
in the monumental splendour of the 'Lyon Chamber', granting audiences in the sumptuous
surroundings of their private apartments, strolling in the pleasure gardens around, perhaps
boating on the loch. Oh to have been there on Twelfth Night (6 January) in the year 1540 when
Sir David Lindsay's epic play *Ane Satyr of the Thrie Estaites* was first performed there
in the presence of James V and his queen, Marie of Guise.
The queens in particular found the palace to their liking and made it their home as often as they
could manage in those peripatetic days. Hence the births there of two sovereigns – James V in 1512,
and Mary Queen of Scots, on 6 December 1542. But the palace holds its tragic memories too. Climb
the north-west turnpike stair and you come to 'Queen Margaret's Bower', the draughty eerie where
it is said Margaret Tudor, James IV's queen, sat in the autumn of 1513 awaiting her husband's return
from war with England; she waited in vain for James was killed at Flodden, in Northumberland.
Over 200 years later Linlithgow was turned into a ruin virtually overnight when in 1746 soldiers
loyal to the Hanoverian George II set alight to the imposing palace of the Stewarts before
marching off to do battle with Prince Charles Edward Stewart's Jacobites at Culloden.
Was it an accident or deliberate sabotage? We will never know.

27 Malleny Garden

This three acre walled garden has a beautiful collection of old-fashioned roses and herbaceous borders, and also houses the National Bonsai Collection for Scotland. A particular feature of the garden is the 400-year-old clipped yew trees, and there is also extensive woodland suitable for a peaceful stroll. The house was built for Sir James Murray around 1635, and its two Georgian reception rooms, added in 1823, are opened by the Friends of Malleny on occasion during the summer.

B2 *Balerno, off the A70 Lanark Road, six miles W of Edinburgh city centre.*

P WC & £

All year, daily, 10am–6pm or dusk if earlier.

Tel 0131 449 2283   www.nts.org.uk

28 Midlothian Snowsports Centre

An artificial ski centre with two main slopes, two nursery slopes and a jump slope, floodlit throughout winter. Ski and snowboard instruction and equipment are provided. Also available is a downhill mountain bike trail, and chairlift which is open to sightseers.

C2 *Hillend on A702, half a mile off Edinburgh City bypass at Lothianburn junction*

P WC A ⚡ 🏃 ♿ ££

Sept–Apr, daily, 9.30am; Sun closes at 7pm.
May–Aug, Mon–Fri, 9.30am–9pm;
Sat–Sun, closes at 7pm.

Tel 0131 445 4433   www.ski.midlothian.gov.uk

29 Muirfield Golf Course

Muirfield, home of the Honourable Company of Edinburgh Golfers, was established in 1744. At 6,601 yards and a par of 73 it is a demanding test and does not conform to the usual rules of classic and seaside links courses. This exclusive club has been host to both the Open Championship and the Ryder Cup. Visitors are restricted to Tuesdays and Thursdays.

F4 *Off A198 at Gullane, E of Edidnburgh*

P WC ✕ 🏛 ♿ £££

Booking Essential

Tel 01620 842123   www.muirfield.org.uk

30 Museum of Flight

Two massive hangars, part of a former RAF airfield, house Scotland's national aviation collection, comprising of aircraft, engines, rockets, photographs, a reference library, archives, models, clothing, instruments and propellers. There are around 50 complete aircraft, from Britain's oldest surviving aeroplane, Percy Pilcher's Hawk glider of 1896, to modern passenger airliners and jet fighters. The collection includes military models, helicopters, microlights, trainers and prototypes, plus exhibits relating to parachuting, ballooning and space flight. The site was the departure point of the airship R34 which made the first east to west crossing of the Atlantic in July 1919, and the collection includes a number of R34 relics. Amongst events held at the museum is the annual vintage and classic vehicle rally in May, and the Festival of Flight in July, with displays by early vintage aeroplanes, modern jets and WW2 aircraft. The Concorde Experience, opened in 2005, tells the story of Concorde G–BOAA. Visitors can see a presentation and pre-book on board tours.

F3 *Twenty miles E of Edinburgh city centre at East Fortune Airfield, on B1347, NE of Haddington.*

P WC & ⚡ 🏛 E 🏛 ♿ ££

Mid Mar–Oct, daily, 10am–5pm.
Nov–mid Mar, weekends only, times vary.
Please check for details.

Tel 01620 880 308   www.nms.ac.uk/flight

31 Myreton Motor Museum

Houses a range of vehicles dating from 1896 to 1969, including cars, motor cycles, bicycles, commercials, military vehicles and interesting ephemera such as period advertising, posters and enamel signs.

F4 *Signposted off A198, three miles E of Aberlady.*

P WC & 🏛 🏛 ££

Apr–Oct, daily, 11am–4pm; Nov–Mar, Sun, 1–3pm.

Tel 01875 870288

32 Newhailes

A palladian house built by the Scottish architect James Smith in 1686, and bought by Sir David Dalrymple of the Scots legal and political dynasty, who made significant improvements and additions to the house. The most significant of these was the library, which played host to many famous figures of the Scottish Enlightenment, and was reportedly described by Dr Johnson as 'the most learned room in Europe'. Much of the original decoration and furnishing has survived intact, and the Trust is working to preserve the house and its contents. The surrounding 18th-century landscape, with its raised walkway and woodland walks, is being gradually restored.

D3 *Off A6095 Newhailes Road, Musselburgh.*

P ⬚ ⬚ ⬚ ⬚ ⬚ ⬚ £££

🕐 House & Visitor Centre: Easter & May–Sept, Thur–Mon, 12 noon–5pm. House by guided tour only: booking advised. Tours run every 30 mins. Estate: all year round, daily, 10am–6pm.

Tel 0131 665 1546 for general enquiries; 0131 653 5599 for bookings   www.nts.org.uk

33 North Berwick Golf Course

Founded in 1832, North Berwick Golf Club is one of Scotland's oldest: players encounter a number of blind shots, ridges across fairways and walls on this classic links of 6,420 yards with a par of 71. Although private, visitors can play at a reasonable fee.

F4 *Off A198, E of Edinburgh*

P ⬚ ✕ ⬚ £££

🕐 Telephone to book.

Tel 01620 892135   www.northberwickgolfclub.com

34 Pentland Hills Regional Park ♣

Designated a park in 1984, the area includes reservoirs, moorland, forestry and farming along with recreational areas and provides activities such as hill-walking, mountain biking and bird-watching. There is also an artifical ski slope (see entry page 78) at Hillend.

C2 *Off the A702 Biggar Road at Glencorse, 7 miles SW of Edinburgh.*

P ⬚ ⬚ ⬚ ⬚ ⬚ ⬚ ⬚

🕐 Park open access.
   Visitor Centre open all year 9.30am-4pm

Tel 01968 677 879   www.edinburgh.gov.uk/phrp

35 Preston Mill and ♨ 🏛
    Phantassie Doocot

A mill has stood on this site since the 16th-century, and the present stone buildings date from the 18th-century. The conical roofed kiln and attractive red painted buildings make

Preston Mill a popular haunt for photographers and artists, while the nearby millpond with resident ducks and geese provides an idyllic countryside spot. The water-wheel and the grain milling machinery it powers are relatively modern and the mill was still used commercially until 1959. Visitors can see and hear the mechanisms in action and learn about the working life of a miller.

G3 *East Linton, off the A1, 23 miles E of Edinburgh.*

P ⬚ ⬚ ⬚ E ⬚ ⬚ ⬚ ££

🕐 Apr–Sept, Thur–Mon, 12 noon–5pm.

Tel 01620 860426   www.nts.org.uk

36 Prestongrange Museum

Coal was first mined here 800 years ago, and the museum, based at a former colliery, tells the story of local industries and the people who worked in them. Free guided tours of the site allow visitors to see a Cornish Beam Engine which once pumped water from the mine, and ride on colliery locomotives on specific 'steam days'. The Power House contains a different temporary exhibition each year.

D3 *Fifteen miles E of Edinburgh on A198 by Prestonpans.*

P ⬚ ⬚ ⬚ E ⬚ ⬚ FREE

🕐 Apr–Oct, daily, 11am–4pm.

Tel 0131 653 2904
www.prestongrangemuseum.org

37 Queensferry Museum

A museum portraying the history of Queensferry, with views across the Forth to the two bridges. An exhibition describes the building of the bridges, the development of the Queensferry Passage and the expansion of the former royal burgh – previously known as the `Queen's Ferry' – in honour of Queen Margaret (1046-1093). It also looks at the annual custom of the Burry Man, who, clad in a costume made from the burrs of the burdock plant, walks through the town on a Friday in early August.

B3 *High Street, South Queensferry, off A90, 12 miles W of Edinburgh.*

⬚ E ⬚ ⬚ FREE

🕐 All year, Mon, Thur, Fri & Sat, 10am–1pm & 2.15–5pm; Sun, 12 noon–5pm.
   Last admission 30 minutes before closing.

Tel 0131 331 5545   www.cac.org.uk

occupies a restored 15th-century doocot next to the churchyard, and visitors can enjoy a short audio-visual dramatisation of the event, and look out over views of the countryside towards the battle site. There is also access to the Parish Church and to the Saltire Memorial where a flag is flown permanently (floodlit at night).

F3 *Athelstaneford, twenty miles E of Edinburgh on A1, turning off at B1347.*

🚾 📺 ☀ FREE

🕐 Apr–Oct, daily, 10am–6pm and St Andrews Day. Tel 01368 863239

38 Rosslyn Chapel ✟

A collegiate church built around 1450 by William Sinclair, Earl of Orkney and Caithness, and Grand Master of the Knights Templar, descendant of the St Clair knights who had settled in Midlothian from France three centuries earlier, stands on the edge of the wooded Esk Valley. The interior is heavy with sculptures and intricate carvings of Biblical stories, and there are many references to the Knights Templar and Freemasonry, along with the famous Apprentice Pillar, a barleycorn-twisted column entwined with foliage rising up from a base of winged serpents, which has its own story to tell. It stands on the edge of the wooded Esk valley and the narrow rocky gorge below with its fast flowing water, gives Rosslyn its name. The wooded glen offers walks and views of the surrounding area.

C2 *Roslin village, six miles S of Edinburgh off A701. Straiton exit from city bypass.*

🅿 🚾 ♿ ☕ 🏛 E 📺 ☀ 👥 🎫 ££

🕐 All year, Mon–Sat, 9.30am–6pm; Sun, 12 noon–4.45pm.

Tel 0131 440 2159   www.rosslynchapel.org.uk

39 Scottish Flag Heritage Centre 🏛

Athelstaneford is the birthplace of Scotland's national flag, the St. Andrew's Cross or Saltire. The flag's origins are associated with a 9th-century battle which took place near this East Lothian village, between an army of Scots/Picts under King Angus and a larger force of Saxons led by Athelstan. Tradition has it that the sudden appearance above the fighting of a white saltire of clouds against the blue sky inspired the Scots/Picts and led them to victory. The date is believed to have been 832 AD. The Flag Centre

40 Scottish Mining Museum 🏛

A mining museum, set inside the restored Lady Victoria Colliery, which describes the highs and lows of an industry that was once the backbone of Scotland. Using a series of interactives, displays, film theatres, magic helmets and a coalface, visitors can see, hear and feel the many different elements that made up this dangerous and sometimes deadly working environment.

D2 *Off the A7 from the E end of the City Bypass at Sheriffhall Roundabout. Follow the signs for Newtongrange and the museum for three miles. Fully wheelchair accessible.*

🅿 🚾 ♿ 👥 ✕ 🏛 E 📺 🎏 ☀ 🎫 🎫 ££

🕐 Feb–Nov, daily, 10am–5pm. Dec–Jan, daily, 10am–4pm.

Tel: 0131 663 7519
www.scottishminingmuseum.com

41 Scottish Seabird Centre ★

The centre enjoys uninterrupted views towards the islands in the Firth of Forth off North Berwick which act as a haven for over 150,000 nesting seabirds. Remote control cameras observe close-up live images of wildlife from the protected offshore islands and their surrounding water, including over 100,000 gannets on the Bass Rock, along with puffins, guillemots, fulmars, shags and kittiwakes. A camera on the Isle of May, a National Nature Reserve and Site of Special Scientific Interest with 40,000 occupied puffin burrows, screens images of seabird colonies along the west facing cliff ledges. A dolphin watch has also been set up from the centre to record sightings and track the bottlenose dolphins which are believed to come from the Moray Firth.

F4 *Harbour front, North Berwick; signposted from Edinburgh on A1.*

Tantallon Castle, East Lothian

P ᵂᶜ ♿ ♨ ✕ ⌂ E ᴬⱽ ⍭ ☀ 劣 ⊞ ££
🕑 All year round, summer 10am–6pm.
　Winter, 10am–4pm; weekends, closes 5.30pm.
Tel 01620 890202　www.seabird.org

42 Tantallon Castle　⏣ 🏰

Set dramatically on cliffs edging the Firth of
Forth, Tantallon Castle has suffered a turbulent
history. Originally built in the 14th-century,
it featured huge 50 ft walls with an imposing
set of towers. Much fought over, it was
strengthened during the 16th-century, but
eventually set into ruins by Cromwell's army
in 1651. Used as the location for the
Childrens TV series *Shoebox Zoo*.

G4　*Three miles E of North Berwick off the A198.*

P ᵂᶜ ♿ ⌂ E ☀ £
🕑 Apr–Sept, daily, 9.30am–6.30pm.
　Oct–Mar, Sat–Wed, 9.30am–4.30pm
Tel 01620 892727　www.historic–scotland.gov.uk

43 Townhill Country Park　♣

Footpaths take walkers round Town Loch
and through Townhill Wood, a mixed woodland
with a variety of wildlife.

B4　*Two miles N of Dunfermline*

P ♿ ⍭ 劣 FREE

🕑 All year round, daily, daylight hours.
Tel 01383 725596

44 Vogrie Country Park　♣

A country park featuring seven miles of
woodland walks, some of which follow the River
Tyne and its rich grasslands, plus an adventure
play area, sculptures and a garden centre.

E2　*Take A68 through Dalkeith, and turn off on B6372
before Pathead. Continue through Dewarton Park
on left.*

P ᵂᶜ ♿ ♨ ⌂ E ⍭ ☀ 劣 £
🕑 Dawn-dusk.
Tel 01875 821990

45 Whitekirk Golf Course　⚑₁₈

The relatively new course at Whitekirk,
established in 1995, sits high on the hill
above North Berwick and enjoys fine views
across the Firth of Forth. The layout of 6,520
yards with a par of 71 is demanding with
its natural water hazards and elevated tees.

F4　*Off A198 at Whitekirk, near North Berwick,
E of Edinburgh*

P ᵂᶜ ✕ ⌂ ⊞ £££
🕑 Booking recommended
Tel 01620 870300　www.whitekirk.com

GENERAL INFORMATION

TRAVEL INFORMATION

Traveline Scotland
Tel: 0870 608 2608

Traveline has information for all local public transport services, including train, bus and coach companies in Edinburgh and the Lothians. They produce a free map of the routes and times of all the major bus companies. Traveline also has details for people travelling with disabilities.

AIRPORT INFORMATION

Edinburgh Airport is located 13km west of the city centre, with good road access. A regular bus service operates from Waverley Bridge to the airport.

BAA Edinburgh
Edinburgh Airport
Edinburgh
EH12 9DN
Tel: 0870 040 0007
Web: www.baa.com

RAIL

The main railway station, Waverley, is located alongside the east end of Princes Street. Leave the train at Haymarket station for the west end of Edinburgh.

Edinburgh Waverley Station
Waverley Bridge
Tel: 08457 484950

Haymarket Station
Haymarket Terrace
Tel: 08457 484950

TRAINS

National Rail Enquiries
Tel: 08457 484950

Great North Eastern
Railway Ltd (GNER)
Station Road
York, YO7 6HT
Tel: General Sales and
Enquiries: 08457 225 225
Customer Assistance:
08457 225 444
*(including disabled traveller
arrangements)*
Customer Relations:
08457 225 333
Web: www.gner.co.uk
Email: customercare@gner.co.uk
**Route:operates along Britain's
East Coast mainline linking
England and Scotland**

First ScotRail
Caledonian Chambers
87 Union Street
Glasgow G1 3TA
Tel: Fares & Train Times:
08457 484950
Telesales: 08457 550033
Customer Relations:
0845 601 5929
Web: www.firstscotrail.co.uk
**Routes: operates within
Scotland and also Caledonian
Sleepers, which link Aberdeen,
Edinburgh, Fort William,
Glasgow and Inverness with
London**

Virgin Trains
Suite 3/1, Queens House,
19 St Vincent Place
Glasgow G1 2DT
Web: www.virgintrains.co.uk
**Routes: operates between
London Euston–Scotland**

BUSES AND COACHES

Edinburgh has a good network of bus routes. Details of the route the bus is taking are displayed on the front of the bus. The driver issues tickets for each journey, the exact amount is generally required. Passes for unlimited travel on a daily or weekly basis are also available. Further details and timetables can be obtained from tourist information centres or by contacting the individual bus companies.

First
14-16 Erskine Road
Dalkeith EH22 1HH
Tel: 0131 225 3858
Web: www.firstgroup.com
**Routes include: Edinburgh City
Centre, Edinburgh-Falkirk,
Edinburgh-Kelso, Edinburgh-
Livingstone, Edinburgh-Stirling**

Lothian Buses PLC
Head Office
55 Annadale Street
Edinburgh, EH7 4AZ

Travel Centres at Hanover Street, Shandwick Place and Waverley Bridge
Tel: 0131 555 6363
Web: www.lothianbuses.co.uk
Email: info@lothianbuses.co.uk
**Routes: Edinburgh and the
Lothians Also operates
Edinburgh Tour (City
sightseeing) Airlink (shuttle
service between Edinburgh
Airport and the city centre)
and Britannia (link between**

the city centre and the Royal Yacht Britannia) Edinburgh Bus Station is located in Elder Street, adjoining the new shopping centre.

COACHES

Scottish Citylink Coaches Limited
Buchanan Bus Station
Killermont Street
Glasgow, G2 3NP
Tel: 08705 505050
Web: www.citylink.co.uk

Routes: Edinburgh-Aberdeen, Edinburgh-Dundee, Edinburgh-Glasgow, Edinburgh-Inverness, Edinburgh-Isle of Skye, Edinburgh-Glasgow-Stranraer-Belfast

TAXIS

Taxis in the city are usually plentiful and the majority will take wheelchairs. They can be hailed in the street, picked up at various ranks or phoned. Listed below are the phone numbers of some of the most widely used companies:

Accolade City Cars
Tel: 0131 557 5718

Central Radio Taxis
Tel: 0131 229 2468

Computer Cabs
Tel: 0131 228 2555

City Cabs
Tel: 0131 228 1211

CAR HIRE

Arnold Clark Car and Van Rental
Tel: 0845 607 4500
Web: www.arnoldclark.co.uk

Avis Rent a Car
Edinburgh Airport
Tel: 0131 344 3900
Web: www.avis.co.uk

Belmont Peugeot
Tel: 0131 453 6644
Web: www.jmgroup.co.uk

Capital Car and Van Hire
Tel: 0131 652 9898
Web: www.121carhire.com

Condor Self Drive Hire
Tel: 0131 229 6333
Web: www.condorselfdrive.co.uk

Enterprise Rent-A-Car
Tel: 0131 442 4400
Web: www.enterprise.com

Ford Rent-A-Car
Tel: 0131 557 0000
Web: www.rent-ford.com

Good News Car Hire
Tel: 0131 442 4400
Email: operations@goodnewsselfdrive.com

Gran Turismo
Tel: 0131 466 3447
Web: www.granturismo.demon.co.uk

Thrifty Car Rental
Tel: 0131 337 1319
Web: www.thrifty.co.uk

Road and weather information for all of Scotland is available from NADICS on www.nadics.org.uk and the AA Roadwatch and Weatherwatch.
Tel: 09003 401 100
www.theaa.com

Forth Road Bridge
Tel: 0131 319 1699

Forth Road Bridge Toll Charges for cars are £1 and are charged only for those travelling in a northbound direction.

PARKING

The City of Edinburgh Council provides approximately 5,000 pay and display on-street parking spaces in the city, alternative off street parking is also available throughout the city.

CYCLE WAYS

There is a good range of cycle lanes marked throughout the city, contact Traveline Scotland for more information. A local pressure group, SPOKES, publishes a citywide map of cycleways, available in cycle shops, book shops or online at www.spokes.org.uk. Bikes are also available for hire.

National Cycle Network
Sustrans Scotland
16a Randolph Crescent
Edinburgh, EH3 7TT
Tel: 0131 539 8122
Web: www.sustrans.co.uk
Email: info@sustrans.co.uk

WALKING

Walking tours are very popular and are organised by several groups. Information can be found at the Tourist Information Centres and the groups often advertise by placard at their starting points, for example in the High Street. They include ghost tours along the Royal Mile, some of which are held at night.

Edinburgh is also fortunate in having country walks starting at its very centre in Holyrood Park along with country parks that have footpaths and trails just a short journey from the city.

EMERGENCY
In an emergency call the Operator - 999 for fire, police or ambulance. Calls are free from any telephone.

PLEASE NOTE:
When telephoning from Edinburgh, omit 0131 from all numbers. Addresses are all Edinburgh unless stated otherwise.

POLICE
Police Stations are located throughout the city.

Lothian & Borders Police HQ
Fettes Ave
EH4 1RB
Tel: 0131 311 3131

British Transport Police
Tel: 0800 405040

LOST PROPERTY
Enquire at the nearest police station or contact the following:

Police
Tel: 0131 226 6966

Waverley Station
Tel: 0131 550 2333

First ScotRail
Tel: 0141 335 3276

Virgin Trains
Tel: 0870 789 1234

Lothian Buses
Tel: 0131 558 8858

POST OFFICES
Post offices are generally open Monday-Friday 9am–5.30pm, Saturday 9am–12 noon and closed Sunday, some smaller post offices maybe closed between 1pm and 2pm for lunch and one afternoon mid-week.

CITY CENTRE
8-10 St James Centre
EH1 3SR
Tel: 0131 556 0478

7 Hope Street
EH2 4EN
Tel: 0131 886 6823

40 Frederick Street
EH2 1EY
Tel: 0131 226 6937

South Gyle Post Office
47 South Gyle Avenue
EH12 9JU
Tel: 0131 317 1191

Royal Mail
102 West Port
EH3 9HS
Tel: 0131 228 7200

Post Office Counters Helpline:
Tel: 0345 223344

MEDICAL INFORMATION
**For emergencies:
dial 999 - for fire, police or ambulance. Calls are free from any telephone.**

For an ordinary illness or a minor accident, your hotel or place of residence can usually put you in touch with a local doctor or dentist.
For dental emergencies out of hours, contact the Western General Hospital.

Late-opening chemist;
Boots
48 Shandwick Place
EH2 4SA
Tel: 0131 225 6757

HOSPITALS
City Hospital
51 Green Bank Drive
EH10 5SB
Tel: 0131 536 6000

Eastern General Hospital
Seafield Street
EH6 7LN
Tel: 0131 536 7000

Edinburgh Dental Hospital
1 Lauriston Place
EH3 9YW
Tel: 0131 536 4900

Royal Edinburgh Hospital
Morningside Terrace
EH10 5HF
Tel: 0131 537 6000

Royal Hospital for Sick Children
9 Sciennes Road
EH9 1LF
Tel: 0131 536 0000

Royal Infirmary of Edinburgh
Little France
Old Dalkeith Road
EH16 4SU
Tel: 0131 536 1000

Western General Hospital
NHS Trust
Crewe Road South
EH4 2XU
Tel: 0131 537 1000

CATERING FOR DISABILITY IN SCOTLAND
Scotland welcomes visitors with disabilities. There are a number of organisations designed to aid visitors who need advice and information on visiting Scotland.

Capability Scotland is Scotland's primary disability organisation and can offer help and advise for visitors to Scotland. For further information please contact:
Advice Service Capability Scotland (ASCS)
11 Ellersley Road
Edinburgh, EH12 6 HY
Tel: 0131 313 5510
Web:
www.capability-scotland.org.uk
Email:
ascs@capability-scotland.org.uk

Holiday Care is a national charity and the UK's principal provider of travel advice and information for disabled people and their carers. For further information contact:

Holiday Care
7th Floor
Sunley House
4 Bedford Park
Croydon, Surrey
CR0 2AP
Tel: 0845 1249971
Web: www.holidaycare.org.uk
Email: info@holidaycare.org

Tripscope also provides information on any aspect of local or national transport for people with disabilities. For further information contact:

Tripscope
The Vassall Centre
Gill Avenue
Bristol
BS16 2QQ
Tel: 0845 758 5641
Web: www.tripscope.org.uk
Email:
enquiries@tripscope.org.uk

USEFUL ADDRESSES
VisitScotland
Ocean Point One
94 Ocean Drive, Leith
Edinburgh EH6 6JH
Tel: 0131 332 2433
Web: www.visitscotland.com
Email: info@visitscotland.com

Historic Scotland
Longmore House
Salisbury Place
Edinburgh
EH9 1SH
Tel: 0131 668 8600
Web:
www.historic-scotland.gov.uk
Email:
hsexplorer@scotland.gov.uk

The National Trust for Scotland
Wemyss House
28 Charlotte Square
EH2 4ET
Tel: 0131 243 9300
Web: www.nts.org.uk
Email: information@nts.org.uk

Ramblers Association
(Scottish Office)
Kingfisher House
Auld Mart Business Park
Milnathort
Kinross
KY13 9DA
Tel: 01577 861222
Web: www.ramblers.org.uk
Email:enquiries
@scotland.ramblers.org.uk

Royal Society for the Protection of Birds
Scotland Headquarters
Dunedin House
25 Ravelston Terrace
EH4 3TP
Tel: 0131 311 6500
Web: www.rspb.org.uk
Email:
rspb.scotland@rspb.org.uk

Scottish Natural Heritage
12 Hope Terrace
EH9 2AS
Tel: 0131 447 4784
Web: www.snh.org.uk
Email: enquiries@snh.gov.uk

Scottish Wildlife Trust
Cramond House
Cramond Glebe Road
EH4 6NS
Tel: 0131 312 7765
Web: www.swt.org.uk
Email: enquiries@swt.org.uk

Scottish Youth Hostel
Association
7 Glebe Crescent
Stirling
FK8 2JA
Tel: 01786 891400
Web: www.syha.org.uk
Email: info@syha.org.uk

CARAVAN & CAMPING SITES
Drum Mohr Caravan Park
Levenhall,
Musselburgh
EH21 8JS
Tel: 0131 665 6867
Web: www.drummohr.org
Email: bookings@drummohr.org

Mortonhall Caravan Park
Frogston Road East
EH16 6TJ
Tel: 0131 664 1533
Web: www.meadowshead
.co.uk/mortonhall

Edinburgh Caravan Club Site
Marine Drive
EH4 5EN
Tel: 0131 312 6874

ACCOMMODATION
Information and reservations for Hotels, Guest Houses and B & Bs can be obtained from the Tourist Information Centres on page 5

YOUTH HOSTELS
The Scottish Youth Hostel Association has two properties open all year in Edinburgh, with three more open from July to September.
The SYHA can be contacted on 0870 155 32 55.
Hostel accommodation can also be booked through Tourist Information Centres.
SYHA website: www.syha.org.uk

Bruntsfield Youth Hostel
7 Bruntsfield Crescent
EH10
Tel: 0131 447 2994

Eglinton Youth Hostel
18 Eglinton Crescent
EH12 5DD
Tel: 01131 337 1120

BANKS AND BUREAU DE CHANGE

Most of the banks in the city will exchange foreign currency. Normal banking hours are 09.30–16.30.

Bureau de Change - outside bank hours:

Tourist Information Centre
3 Princes Street
Tel: 0845 22 55 121

Waverley Station
Tel: 0131 557 2784

Edinburgh Airport
Tel: 0131 333 3146

American Express
139 Princes Street
Tel: 0131 718 2501

Thomas Cook
52 Hanover Street
Tel: 0131 226 5500

26-28 Frederick Street
Tel: 0131 465 7700

Cameron Toll Shopping Centre
Unit 13B, Lady Road
Tel: 0131 465 7600

Unit 37 Gyle Shopping Centre
60 South Gyle Broadway
Tel: 01456 8000

BANKS

Abbey National plc
31 Hanover Street
Tel: 0845 765 4321

Alliance & Leicester plc
136 Princes Street
Tel: 0131 225 4253

Allied Irish Bank
19 Charlotte Square
Tel: 0131 226 5206

Bank of Ireland
Edinburgh Business Centre
11-13 Castle Street
Tel: 0131 220 6686

Bank Of Scotland
The Mound
Tel: 0845 600 0180

Barclays Bank plc
1 St Andrews Square
Tel: 0845 600 0180

Bradford & Bingley
20 Frederick Street
Tel: 0131 225 7357

Bristol West plc
13a Castle Street
Tel: 0131 220 6022

Cheltenham & Gloucester plc
19 Castle Street
Tel: 0131 226 2696

Citibank N.A.
Capital House
2 Festival Square
Tel: 0131 228 3000

Clydesdale Bank
20 Hanover Street
Tel: 08457 826302

Halifax plc
75 George Street
Tel: 0845 677010

HFC Bank plc
57 Frederick Street
Tel: 0131 226 4471

HSBC Bank plc
76 Hanover Street
Tel: 0131 456 3290

Lloyds TSB Scotland
28 Hanover Street
Tel: 0845 300 2550

Royal Bank of Scotland plc
36 St Andrews Square
Tel: 0131 556 8555

Woolwich plc
72-74 George Street
Tel: 0845 071 8220

BUILDING SOCIETIES

Britannia Building Society
55 George Street
0131 225 7283

Century Building Society
21 Albany Street
Tel: 0131 556 1711

Dunfermline Building Society
3 South Charlotte Street
Tel: 0131 225 3231

Nationwide Building Society
71 George Street
Tel: 0131 456 1000

Newcastle Building Society
63-65 Shandwick Place
Tel: 0131 229 2977

Scottish Building Society
23 Manor Place
Tel: 0131 220 1111

Skipton Building Society
19 Frederick Street
Tel: 0131 225 2715

Yorkshire Building Society
46 Hanover Street
Tel: 0845 120 0100

CONSULATES IN EDINBURGH

American Consulate General
3 Regent Terrace
EH7 5BW
Tel: 0131 556 8315

Australian Consulate
69 George Street
EH2 2HN
Tel: 0131 624 3333

Austrian Consulate
9 Howard Place
EH3 5JZ
Tel: 0131 558 1955

Canadian Consulate
Burness
50 Lothian Road
EH3 9WJ
Tel: 0131 473 6320

Consulate General of the Peoples Republic of China
55 Corstorphine Road
EH12 5QG
Tel: 0131 337 9896

Czech Republic Consulate
12a Riselaw Cresent
EH10 6HL
Tel: 0131 447 9509

The Danish Consulate
48 Melville Street
EH3 7HF
Tel: 0131 220 5528

Finnish Consulate General
11 Randolph Crescent
EH3 7TT
Tel: 0131 225 7954

French Consulate General
11 Randolph Crescent
EH3 7TT
Tel: 0131 225 7954

German Consulate General
16 Eglinton Crescent
EH12 5DG
Tel: 0131 337 2323

Icelandic Consulate
45 Queen Street
EH2 3NH
Tel: 0131 220 5775

Consulate General of India
17 Rutland Square
EH1 2BB
Tel: 0131 229 2144

Consulate General of Ireland
16 Randolph Crescent
EH3 7TT
Tel: 0131 226 7711

Italian Consulate General
32 Melville Street
EH3 7HA
Tel: 0131 226 3631

Japanese Consulate General
2 Melville Crescent
EH3 7HW
Tel: 0131 225 4777

Consular Office of Monaco
39 Castle Street
EH2 3BH
Tel 0131 225 1200

Netherlands Consulate
Thistle Court, 1-2 Thistle Street
EH2 1DD
Tel: 0131 220 3226

New Zealand Consulate
5 Rutland Square
EH1 2AX
Tel: 0131 222 8109

Norwegian Consulate
86 George Street
EH2 3BU
Tel: 0131 226 5701

The Polish Consulate
2 Kinnear Road EH3 5PE
Tel: 0131 552 0301

Russian Consulate General
58 Melville Street
EH3 7HF
Tel: 0131 225 7098

Spanish Consular Agency
63 North Castle Street
EH2 3LJ
Tel: 0131 220 1843

Swedish Consulate General
22 Hanover Street
EH2 2EN
Tel: 0131 220 6050

PLACES OF WORSHIP
Church of Scotland
St Giles Cathedral, High Street
Tel: 0131 225 9442
www.stgiles.net

Greyfriars Tolbooth and Highland Kirk
Greyfriars Place
Tel: 0131 225 5429
www.greyfrairskirk.com

Parish Church of St Cuthbert
5 Lothian Road
Tel: 0131 229 1142
www.st-cuthberts.net

St Andrew's and St George's
George Street, Edinburgh
Tel: 0131 25 3847
www.standrewsand
stgeorges.org.uk

Scottish Episcopal
St Mary's Cathedral
Palmerston Place
Tel: 0131 225 6293
www.cathedral.net

St John's
Princes Street
Tel: 0131 229 7565
www.stjohns-edinburgh.org.uk

Roman Catholic
St Mary's Metropolitan Cathedral
Broughton Street
Tel: 0131 556 1798
www.stmaryscathedral.co.uk

St Patrick's Church
Cowgate
Tel 0131 556 1973
www.stpatricksparish.co.uk

Methodist
Central Hall
2 West Tollcross
Tel: 0131 221 9029

Baptist
Charlotte Chapel
West Rose Street
Tel: 0131 225 4812
www.charlottechapel.org

Free Church of Scotland
Buccleuch and Greyfriars
West Crosscauseway &
Buccleuch Street
Tel: 0131 667 0867
www.buccleuchfreechurch.co.uk

Jewish
Edinburgh Hebrew Congregation
4 Salisbury Road
Tel: 0131 667 3144
www.ehcong.com

Islamic
Central Mosque
50 Potterrow
Tel: 0131 667 1777
www.icetrust.org

Pakistan Association
Mosque Centre
11 Pilrig Street
Tel: 0131 554 9904

Orthodox
Orthodox Community and
Chaplaincy of St Andrew
2 Meadow Lane
Tel: 0131 667 0372

Quaker
Society of Friends Quaker
Meeting House
7 Victoria Terrace
Tel: 0131 225 4825

Salvation Army
1 East Adam Street
Tel: 0131 667 4313

FESTIVALS AND EVENTS

APRIL

EDINBURGH INTERNATIONAL SCIENCE FESTIVAL
various venues, Edinburgh

MAY

CAPITAL BLUES FESTIVAL
Corn Exchange

JUNE

MEADOWS FESTIVAL

GARDENING SCOTLAND, The Royal Caledonian Horticultural Society, Ingliston

JULY

FESTIVAL OF FLIGHT
East Fortune, East Lothian

LINLITHGOW RENAISSANCE FESTIVAL
Linlithgow, West Lothian

AUGUST

EDINBURGH MILITARY TATTOO
Edinburgh Castle

NORTH BERWICK HIGHLAND GAMES
North Berwick

EDINBURGH FESTIVAL CAVALCADE
City Centre, Edinburgh

DECEMBER

WINTER WONDERLAND
East Princes Street Gardens

ITALIAN FILM FESTIVAL
Filmhouse, Edinburgh

BELTANE FIRE FESTIVAL
Calton Hill

HADDINGTON FESTIVAL
Haddington, East Lothian

EDINBURGH INTERNATIONAL CHILDREN'S FESTIVAL, various venues, Edinburgh

LINLITHGOW RIDING OF THE MARCHES
Linlithgow, West Lothian

ROYAL HIGHLAND SHOW
Royal Highland Centre, Ingliston

HONEST TOUN'S FESTIVAL
Musselburgh, East Lothian

INTERNATIONAL JAZZ AND BLUES FESTIVAL
various venues, Edinburgh

EDINBURGH FESTIVAL, end July-beginning September, various venues

EDINBURGH FESTIVAL FRINGE
various venues

EDINBURGH INTERNATIONAL BOOK FESTIVAL Charlotte Square

EDINBURGH INTERNATIONAL FILM FESTIVAL
Filmhouse

EDINBURGH INTERNATIONAL FESTIVAL
various venues

EDINBURGH'S HOGMANAY
various venues

EDINBURGH FESTIVAL

end July-beginning September

In 1947, post-war Edinburgh hosted its first International Festival. Since then, the festival has evolved into one of the largest arts festivals in the world, attracting over 100,000 visitors a year. Music, drama, literature and film have, over the years, become an intrinsic part of the summer in Scotland's historic capital.

EDINBURGH INTERNATIONAL FESTIVAL

The UK's annual premier arts festival provides visitors with a unique opportunity to experience a variety of international theatre, dance, opera and music.

Contact: The Hub
Castlehill, Royal Mile, Edinburgh, EH1 2NE
Tel: 0131 473 2099   www.eif.co.uk

EDINBURGH FESTIVAL FRINGE

For three weeks every August, Edinburgh is host to the largest arts festival in the world. From comedy to magic, over 1000 shows are performed a day at more than 200 venues across the city

Contact: Edinburgh Fringe Festival
180 High Street, Edinburgh, EH1 1QS
Tel: 0131 226 0026   www.edfringe.com

THE EDINBURGH MILITARY TATTOO

Staged on the esplanade of Edinburgh's historic castle, this annual military spectacle combines music and dance with drama and pageantry.

Contact: Tattoo Office
32 Market Street, Edinburgh, EH1 1QB
Tel: 0131 225 1188   www.edintattoo.co.uk

EDINBURGH INTERNATIONAL BOOK FESTIVAL

Attracting bibliophiles from around the world, the annual Book Festival encompasses a wide range of activities such as readings, demonstrations and workshops, author interviews and literary seminars.

Contact: Scottish Book Centre
137 Dundee Street, Edinburgh, EH11 1BG
Tel: 0131 228 5444   www.edbookfest.co.uk

EDINBURGH INTERNATIONAL FILM FESTIVAL

Established in 1947, the Film Festival annually showcases over 300 films, including a number of world premiers.

Contact: Edinburgh International Film Festival
88 Lothian Road,
Edinburgh, EH3 9BZ
Tel: 0131 228 4051   www.edfilmfest.org.uk

EDINBURGH INTERNATIONAL JAZZ & BLUES FESTIVAL

Stages in a number of venues across Edinburgh, visitors can enjoy a wide range of Scottish and International jazz and blues

Contact: Edinburgh International Jazz Festival
29 St Stephen Street, EH3 5AN
Tel: 0131 225 2202
www.edinburghjazzfestival.co.uk

EDINBURGH INTERNATIONAL SCIENCE FESTIVAL

The Science Festival offers over 70 events in major venues throughout the city during April. 12 days of educational and interactive entertainment for all the family

Contact: Edinburgh International Science Festival
4 Gayfield Place Lane,
Edinburgh,
EH1 3NZ
Tel: 0131 558 7666   www.sciencefestival.co.uk

EDINBURGH INTERNATIONAL CHILDREN'S FESTIVAL

A festival for children in May, that brings world famous theatre productions to Edinburgh.

Contact: Imaginate
45a George Street, Edinburgh, EH2 2HT
Tel: 0131 225 8050   www.imaginate.org.uk
Email: info@imaginate.org.uk

Various other festivals and events take place in Edinburgh throughout the year, contact the Tourist Information Centre for further details.

ENTERTAINMENT

THEATRES & CONCERT HALLS
(Box Office numbers)

Assembly rooms,
George Street
Tel: 0131 220 4349
www.assemblyrooms
edinburgh.co.uk

Bedlam Theatre
11B Bristo Place
Tel: 0131 225 9873
www.bedlamfringe.co.uk

Brunton Theatre
Ladywell Way
Musselburgh
Tel: 0131 665 2240
www.bruntontheatre.co.uk

Church Hill Theatre
33 Morningside Road
Tel: 0131 447 7597

Edinburgh Festival Theatre
13-29 Nicholson Street
Tel: 0131 529 6000
www.eft.co.uk

Edinburgh Playhouse
18-22 Greenside Place
Tel: 0870 606 3424

King's Theatre
2 Leven Street
Tel: 0131 529 6000
www.eft.co.uk

Netherbow Arts Centre
43-45 High Street
Tel: 0131 556 9579

Queen's Hall
37 Clerk Street
Tel: 0131 668 2019
www.thequeenshall.net

Reid Concert Hall
Bristo Square
Tel: 0131 650 2019

Ross Open Air Theatre
Princes Street Gardens
Tel: 0131 228 8616

Royal Lyceum Theatre Company
Grindlay Street (off Lothian Road)
Edinburgh
Tel: 0131 248 4848
www.lyceum.org.uk

St Cecilia's Hall
Niddrie Street
Tel: 0131 650 2423

Theatre Workshop
34 Hamilton Place
Tel: 0131 226 5425
www.theatreworkshop.co.uk

Traverse Theatre
Cambridge Street
Edinburgh
Tel: 0131 228 1404
www.traverse.co.uk

Usher Hall
Lothian Road
Edinburgh
Tel: 0131 228 8616
www.usherhall.co.uk

COMEDY
The Stand Comedy Club
5 York Place
Edinburgh
Tel: 0131 558 7272
www.thestand.co.uk

CINEMAS
Odeon
120 Lothian Road
& Wester Hailes
Tel: 0870 505 0007
www.odeon.co.uk

Cameo Cinema
38 Home Street
Tel: 0131 228 4141
www.picturehouse.co.uk

Dominion Cinema
Newbattle Terrace
Tel: 0131 447 2660
www.dominioncinemas.net

Filmhouse
88 Lothian Road
Edinburgh
Tel: 0131 228 2688
www.filmhousecinema.com

UGC Cinemas Megaplex
Fountain Park
Dundee Street
Edinburgh
0870 902 0417
www.ugccinemas.co.uk

UCI Cinemas
7 Kinnaird Park
Newcraighall Road
Tel: 0131 669 0777
www.uci.co.uk

Vue Cinema
Greenside
Tel: 0871 224 0240
www.myvue.com

SHOPPING

Edinburgh has a wide choice of shopping facilities, from historical Princes Street in the heart of the city to the latest addition, Ocean Terminal at Leith.

Princes Street is the main shopping street, which has many standard high street names including Marks & Spencer, BHS and Boots. Department stores include Frasers, Debenhams and the independent Jenners famous for its food hall and traditional clothing. There are also numerous smaller shops to be found, many of them catering for tourists. Above Waverley Station is the Princes Mall, a modern shopping centre with a food-court, built on the site of the old Waverley Market, again with a mixture of well-known outlets and specialist shops. At the east end of Princes Street is the St James Centre which incorporates John Lewis and adjoining the centre in St Andrews Square is the recently opened Harvey Nicholls.

Running parallel to Princes Street is George Street with an assortment of specialist shops, and the narrower Rose Street which is now a pedestrian precinct, again with specialist shops, street cafes, pubs and restaurants. There are numerous other establishments and outlets in the streets emanating from Princes Street.

The Royal Mile in the Old Town, from the High Street down to Canongate, along with Victoria Street, Cockburn Street and the Grassmarket are all areas with specialist shops, cafes, pubs and restaurants, mainly catering for tourists.

There are several shopping centres dotted around the City with good public transport links from the city centre. The Gyle Centre is on the west side of Edinburgh with over 50 retail outlets, a food-court and other services. Cameron Toll Centre lies a few minutes to the south-east of the City Centre and is well serviced by bus routes. Fort Kinnaird Retail Park is a 20 minute bus ride south of the city adjacent to the A1 with well-known retail outlets and an entertainment centre. The newest shopping centre is Ocean Terminal at Leith. The centre contains high street names, along with restaurants, bars and a cinema. The Royal Yacht *Britannia* is berthed alongside the complex, which has been designed to feel like a cruise ship. Again there are good bus links from the city centre.

SHOPPING CENTRES

PRINCES MALL
Princes Street
Tel: 0131 557 3759
www.princesmall-edinburgh.co.uk
Open: Mon–Wed, Fri & Sat, 9am–6pm;
Thur, 9am–7pm; Sun, 11am–5pm

ST JAMES SHOPPING CENTRE
Leith Street
Tel: 0131 557 0050
www.stjamesshopping.com
Open: Mon–Wed, Fri & Sat, 9am–6pm;
Thur, 9am–8pm; Sun, 11am–5pm

CAMERON TOLL SHOPPING CENTRE
6 Lady Road, South Edinburgh
Tel: 0131 666 2777
www.camerontoll.co.uk
Open: Mon–Sat, 7.30am–10pm; Sun, 8am–8pm

FORT KINNAIRD RETAIL PARK
Kinnaird Park
Tel: 0131 669 4784   www.fortkinnaird.com
Open: From 9am–closing times vary

GYLE SHOPPING CENTRE
101 Edinburgh Park
Tel: 0131 539 9000
www.gyleshopping.com
Open: Mon–Fri, 8.30am–10pm;
Sat, 8am–8pm; Sun, 9am–8pm

OCEAN TERMINAL
Ocean Drive, Leith
Tel: 0131 555 8888
www.oceanterminal.com
Open: Mon–Fri, 10am–8pm; Sat, 10am–7pm;
Sun, 11am–6pm. Bars, restaurant and
cinema open until midnight.

SPORTING AND LEISURE VENUES

ACTIVITIES
Absolutely Scotland
Tel: 0870 240 1380
www.absolutely-scotland.co.uk

Bedlam Events
Tel: 07000 233526
www.bedlam.co.uk

Laserquest
Tel: 0131 346 1919

Mavis Hall Park
Tel: 01875 833733
www.mavishallpark.co.uk

Outdoor Scotland
Tel: 0131 555 2414
www.outdoorscotland.co.uk

Skirmish Paintball Games
Tel: 0800 052 6190

ANGLING
Markle Fisheries
Tel: 01620 867213

Morton Fishery
Tel: 01506 882293
www.mortonfishery.co.uk

ARCHERY
Cluny Clays Centre
Tel: 01592 720374
www.clunyclays.co.uk

Mavis Park Hall
Tel: 01875 833733
www.mavishallpark.co.uk

Scottish Archery Centre
Tel: 01620 850401
www.scottisharcherycentre.co.uk

BALLOONING
Alba Ballooning
Tel: 0131 667 4251
www.albaballooning.co.uk

CLIMBING
The Adventure Centre
Tel: 0131 229 3919
www.adventurescotland.com

Meadowbank Sports Centre
Tel: 0131 661 5351

Outdoor Scotland
Tel: 0131 555 2414
www.outdoorscotland.co.uk

CYCLING
Bike Trax Cycle Hire
Tel: 0131 228 6633
www.biketrax.co.uk

Law Cycles Bike Hire
Tel: 01620 890643
www.lawcycles.co.uk

Great bikes, no bull
Tel: 0131 467 7775
www.greatbikesnobull.com

GOLF
Baberton
Tel: 0131 453 3361

Bathgate Golf Club
Tel: 01506 630505
www.bathgategolfclub.visps.com

Braid Hills Golf Course
Tel: 0131 447 6666

Broomieknowe
Tel: 0131 663 9317

Bruntsfield Links Golfing Society
See separate entry

Carrick Knowe Golf Course
Tel: 0131 337 1096

Castle Park Golf Club
Tel: 01620 810733
www.castleparkgolfclub.co.uk

Craigentinny Golf Course
Tel: 0131 554 7501

Craigmillar Park Golf Club
Tel: 0131 667 0047

Dalmahoy
Tel: 0131 333 4105

Deer Park Golf & Country Club
Tel: 01506 431037

Duddingston
Tel: 0131 661 7688

East Lothian Golf Range
Tel: 01875 616 100

Gifford Golf Club
Tel: 01620 810267

Glencorse Golf Range
Tel: 0131 440 4200

Gogarburn Golf Club
Tel: 0131 333 4718

Greenburn Golf Club
Tel: 01501 770292

Gullane
See separate entry
www.gullanegolfclub.com

Haddington Golf Course
Tel: 01620 823627

Harburn Golf Club
Tel: 01506 871131

Kilspindie Golf Club
Tel: 01875 870358

Kings Acre Golf Course
& Academy
Tel: 0131 663 3456
www.kings-acregolf.com

Kingsknowe
Tel: 0131 441 1144

Liberton
Tel: 0131 664 3009

Linlithgow Golf Club
Tel: 01506 842585
www.linlithgowgolf.co.uk

Longniddry
Tel: 01875 852141

Lothianburn Golf Club
Tel: 0131 445 2206

Melville Golf Centre
Tel: 0131 663 8083
www.melvillegolf.co.uk

Mortonhall
Tel: 0131 447 2411

Muirfield
See separate entry

Murrayfield
Tel: 0131 337 1009

Musselburgh Links
Tel: 0131 665 2005
www.musselburgholdlinks.co.uk

North Berwick
See separate entry
www.topweb.free-
online.co.uk/nb

Portobello Golf Course
Tel: 0131 669 4361

Prestonfield
See separate entry
www.prestonfieldgolfclub.co.uk

Ravelston
Tel: 0131 315 2486

Royal Burgess Golfing Society
See separate entry
www.royalburgess.co.uk

Royal Musselburgh
Tel: 01875 810276

Rutherford Castle Golf Club
Tel: 01968 661233
www.ruth-castlegc.co.uk

Silverknowes Golf Course
Tel: 0131 336 3843

Torphin Hill
Tel: 0131 441 1100

Uphall
Tel: 01506 856404

Vogrie Golf Course
Tel: 01875 821716

West Lothian Golf Club
Tel: 01506 825060

Whitekirk Golf Course
See separate entry
www.whitekirk.com

HORSE RACING
Musselburgh Racecourse
Tel: 0131 665 2859
www.musselburgh-
racecourse.co.uk

HORSE RIDING
Pentland Hills Icelandics
Tel: 01968 661095
www.phicelandics.co.uk

KARTING
Racing Karts
Tel: 01506 410123
www.racingkarts.co.uk

MOTORSPORTS
Cluny Clays Centre
Tel: 01592 720374
www.clunyclays.co.uk

Fastrax Motorsports
Tel: 01383 880300
www.fastraxoff-road.co.uk

Mavis Hall Park
Tel: 01875 833733
www.mavishallpark.co.uk

Skirmish Limited
Tel: 0800 052 6190

SAILING
Port Edgar Sailing School
& Marina
Tel: 0131 331 3330

SHOOTING
Cluny Clays Centre
Tel: 01592 720374
www.clunyclays.co.uk

Mavis Park Hall
Tel: 01875 833733
www.mavishallpark.co.uk

Skirmish Limited
Tel: 0800 052 6190

SKI-ING
Midlothinan Ski Centre
See separate entry
www.midlothian.gov.uk

**SPORTS CENTRES &
SWIMMING POOLS**
Ainslie Park Leisure Centre
Tel: 0131 551 2400

Aubigny Sports Centre
Tel: 01620 826800

Bathgate Sports Centre
Tel: 01506 776790

Bonnyrigg Leisure Centre
Tel: 0131 663 7579

Bubbles Leisure Pool
Tel: 01506 777870

Dalry Swim Centre
Tel: 0131 313 3964

Glenogle Swim Centre
Tel: 0131 343 6376

Gracemount Leisure Centre
Tel: 0131 658 1940

Jack Kane Sports Centre
Tel: 0131 669 0404

Leith Waterworld
Tel: 0131 555 6000

Linlithgow Leisure Centre
Tel: 01506 775440

Loanhead Leisure Centre
Tel: 0131 440 4516

Loch Centre
Tel: 01875 611081

Meadowbank Sports Centre
Tel: 0131 661 5351

Meadowmill Sports Centre
Tel: 01875 614900

Musselburgh Sports Centre
Tel: 0131 653 6367

Newbattle Swimming Pool
Tel: 0131 663 4485

North Berwick Sports Centre
Tel: 01620 893454

Portobello Swim Centre
Tel: 0131 669 6888

Royal Commonwealth Pool
Tel: 0131 667 7211

Saughton Sports Complex
Tel: 0131 444 0422

Warrender Swim Centre
Tel: 0131 447 0052

STADIUMS
Easter Road Stadium
Tel: 0131 661 2159
www.hibs.co.uk

Murrayfield Stadium
Tel: 0131 346 5000
www.sru.org.uk

Tynecastle Park Stadium
Tel: 0131 200 7200
www.heartsfc.co.uk

TENNIS
Craiglockhart Tennis
& Sports Centre
Tel: 0131 443 0101

WALKING
Edinburgh Southern Orienteering
Association
Tel: 0131 225 7771

Outdoor Scotland
Tel: 0131 555 2414
www.outdoorscotland.co.uk

Walkabout Scotland
Tel: 0131 661 7168
www.walkaboutscotland.
fsnet.co.uk

ATTRACTION INDEX

AROUND EDINBURGH

🏛 Ancient Monument

🐟 Aquarium

🏰 Castle or Historic House

♠ Country Park

⌁ Distillery

❀ Garden

⛳ Golf Course

🏯 Historic Scotland

🏛 Museum/Art Gallery

♛ National Trust for Scotland

🏞 Natural Attraction

🐦 Nature Reserve

🚂 Railway

✝ Religious Building

⛷ Ski/Winter Sport

★ Other Attractions

ALPHABETICAL INDEX

Entries in **bold** indicate photographs

First published in Great Britain in 2004 by
Colin Baxter Photography Limited, Grantown-on-Spey, PH26 3NA, Scotland

w w w . c o l i n b a x t e r . c o . u k

Reprinted 2006

Photographs copyright © Colin Baxter 2004. Text copyright © Colin Baxter Photography 2004.
Special text features written by Chris Tabraham.
Mary King's Close feature text and photograph © Past Forward.
Map on page 68 copyright © 2004 Wendy Price Cartographic Services.
Based on mapping by Hallwag, Kümmerly+Frey AG Switzerland.
Edinburgh city plans copyright © XYZ Digital Map Company 2004.

ISBN 1-84107-323-7

Printed in China.

Front cover photograph: *Edinburgh Military Tattoo*
Back cover photograph: *Edinburgh Castle and City from the west.*